BEER: TASTE THE EVOLUTION IN 50 STYLES

For Jess, Nigel and Granda Tony

NATALYA WATSON
BEER: TASTE THE EVOLUTION IN 50 STYLES

**ILLUSTRATION
BY SARAH GREENO**
KYLE BOOKS

An Hachette UK Company
www.hachette.co.uk

First published in Great Britain in 2020 by
Kyle Books, an imprint of Kyle Cathie Ltd.
Carmelite House
50 Victoria Embankment
London EC4Y 0DZ
www.kylebooks.co.uk

ISBN: 978 0 85783 7219

Distributed in the US by Hachette Book Group,
1290 Avenue of the Americas,
4th and 5th Floors, New York, NY 10104

Distributed in Canada by Canadian Manda Group,
664 Annette St., Toronto, Ontario, Canada M6S 2C8

Publisher: Joanna Copestick
Editor: Isabel Gonzalez-Prendergast
Design and illustrations: Sarah Greeno
Production: Lisa Pinnell

A Cataloguing in Publication record for this title
is available from the British Library

Printed in China

10 9 8 7 6 5 4 3 2 1

CONTENTS

INTRODUCTION

HOW TO
USE THIS BOOK

Thanks for joining me on this journey through the history of beer! Before we get stuck in, I want to give you an idea of our plans.

First, we'll break down beer's four main ingredients – malt, water, hops and yeast – and the brewing process, so we're all on the same page about the importance of each ingredient, along with when and how they're used in the brew.

Then we'll do a quick skim of beer's history, from ancient times to the Industrial Age, where our story picks up. We'll also briefly discuss how beer styles are defined and the style guidelines I've used.

Chapter by chapter, you'll learn about modernization of malt, water, hops and yeast, and the new beer styles that these changes created along the way.

Within every chapter are several short sections, little stepping-stones through beer history, each with a recommended beer to taste. You'll find the beer and brewery name, the beer's style, strength and a few flavour descriptors, then any relevant notes on why this particular beer or brewery was chosen to help bring that section's story to life.

I suggest having the beer by your side while reading (if safe to do so, of course). Pub reading is highly recommended. Or if you've got friends who like beer, why not start a book club to chat through each chapter together? This way the flavours can really jump off the page, courtesy of the glass at hand.

I've tried to recommend beers that best represent each style, while also working to make sure they're not too difficult to find at your local supermarket, bottle shop, or online. There are a few that I recognize are quite regional, but in most cases they're the best example of a certain beer style – as they've helped to create it. If you're really struggling, give me a shout and we'll find an alternative.

I've attempted to keep each section short and sippable, but if you've found a story or a flavour you'd like to learn more about, check out the recommended reading in the back. Or if you're feeling inspired, I've included a dozen of my favourite places to visit that help bring these stories to life even better.

Ready? Turn the page and fill your glass – it's time to taste the evolution of beer.

Cheers, Natalya

PS Here's how to reach me:
cheers@beerwithnat.com

Twitter, Facebook, Instagram:
@beerwithnat

1. MALT 2. WATER 3. HOPS 4. YEAST

INTRODUCTION:
MALT

Malt is shorthand for malted barley, in other words barley grains that have gone through the malting process.

Each barley grain, or kernel, contains stores of starches – energy reserves for growing a new plant – but they're kept under lock and key until conditions are just right for germination. By malting the barley, we can trick the grain into thinking it's time to germinate, making those all-important starches accessible.

The malting process has three steps: the grains are soaked, begin to sprout, then sprouting is stopped by applying heat to dry the grains. If germination continued the grain's energy reserves would be used up by the new plant. By stopping the process, we preserve those starches for brewing with instead.

It's this final step that has the biggest impact on the finished beer. The length of time and the temperature in the kiln (where the grains are dried, then toasted) determines the colour, flavour and how much energy – or fermentable extract – each type of malt contributes to the brew.

Malt is broadly grouped into two categories based on how much fermentable extract it contains: base and specialty.

Base malts have loads of available energy reserves, but they also contain all-important enzymes that allow brewers to put this energy to use.

Enzymes are molecules that help speed up chemical reactions. For storage purposes, plant energy is stored as starch – a long chain of carbohydrates. Yeast, however, can only ferment simple sugars, or short chains. Base malts are rich in starch and the enzymes needed to convert that starch to sugar. This conversion happens during the first step of the brewing process, called mashing.

Here are a few base malts worth knowing:

• Pilsner malt has a light golden hue and gives beers a lightly sweet, grainy note, with flavours of white bread or water cracker

• Pale ale malt is an amber colour and brings flavours like bread crust or biscuit to beer

• Vienna malt is a light copper colour with toasty, nutty notes

Specialty malts, on the other hand, are added just for colour and flavour, not as a sugar source. (The high temperatures they are exposed to in the kiln destroy the enzymes needed for starch conversion.)

These are some popular specialty malts:

- Brown malt gives a deep mahogany colour and rich chocolate flavours

- Black malt is used to darken beer's colour and brings roasted, coffee-like or burned notes

- Crystal, or caramel, malt adds body and a caramel sweetness. (Produced by a special method, these grains are not dried before kilning – so they're roasted wet. The moisture plus the high kilning temperatures causes the sugars in the grains to caramelize. As these sugars are a bit too complex to be fermented by yeast, they remain in the finished beer, making it taste sweeter and fuller.)

It's pretty incredible to think beer gets such a broad range of colours and flavours from one simple grain.

Generally speaking, base malts will make up around 90% of the total grain bill. The last 10% is a mix of specialty malts for colour and flavour – a little of these goes a long way. (This wasn't always the case, of course. Brewers didn't understand the principle of fermentable extract until the late 1700s, when a tool called a hydrometer was invented to help measure the amount of sugar in a solution. In Chapter One, we'll learn how this new tool forever changed the flavour of beer.)

While different varieties of barley exist, from two-row and six-row, to winter and spring, and plenty of individual varietals, like Tipple or Maris Otter, our focus is on the impact of the malting and kilning process on the flavour of the finished beer, less so on the varietal.

Beer can also be brewed with other grains, like malted wheat, oats and rye. Even corn and rice can be added in small quantities. Wheat has a higher protein content than barley, so it adds a fuller body to beer along with a slightly hazy appearance. Similarly, oats add a bit of body, giving the beer a smooth, creamy texture along with a nutty flavour. Rye adds a hint of spice.

Corn and rice are not used to add to, but to thin, the body of beer to keep it light and crisp. Brewers can also add sugar directly to their brews. This won't sweeten up the beer, as the yeast will ferment it. Instead it increases the alcohol content and also helps to thin the body.

Although it's not the most important ingredient by volume in brewing (that's water, which we'll discuss next), malt largely determines a beer's colour, flavour and strength.

INTRODUCTION:
WATER

Of beer's four main ingredients, the one used in the highest volume by far is water. In fact, just over 90% of an average pint of beer is water. With that figure in mind, it's easy to see how water can have an impact on beer's flavour – primarily because of the minerals it contains.

Water chemistry is highly dependent upon location. After rain falls, it travels over various different soils, sands and mineral-rich rock deposits, occasionally picking up compounds like calcium or magnesium that alter the local water profile.

There are two main attributes of water chemistry that determine the beer styles to which water in a particular region is best suited: mineral content and pH.

Mineral content tells us if water is best described as "hard" or "soft", based on the quantity and types of minerals contained. Soft water contains very few minerals, while hard water is mineral-rich.

The types of minerals contained then determine whether that hardness is temporary or permanent. Hardness is considered "temporary" if the minerals can be removed by boiling, while "permanent" hardness requires more complex treatments, like reverse osmosis, to remove minerals.

Water containing calcium carbonate, for example, is temporarily hard and better suited to certain styles of beer than permanently hard water containing calcium sulphate. (You'll learn more about which water source lends itself to which beer style and where it can be found in Chapter Three.)

Beyond mineral content, we need to know if the water is acidic, alkaline or neutral from a measure we call pH. This is key in brewing because the all-important enzymes in the mash (which work to convert malt's starches to sugars) only function within certain pH ranges.

To make things even more complicated, mineral composition can affect water's acidity or alkalinity, but not always. (Yep, water chemistry is rather complex!)

For an idea of how important this information was to brewers, it's probably helpful to know the pH scale was developed by a scientist at a brewery – Søren Sørensen at the Carlsberg Laboratory in Denmark in 1909.

Around this time, our understanding of water chemistry changed more broadly. Brewers learned how to add or remove minerals, altering their local water profile to best fit the styles they wanted to brew instead of being limited by it.

These days, breweries like Guinness can have facilities around the world and brew beer to taste just like it would in Dublin because they can adjust their water chemistry accordingly.

In addition to water chemistry, water supply is important to breweries, as a large amount of water is required for the overall brewing process (much more than the amount that ends up in your pint glass). Process water is used for cleaning, cooling, steam generation and more, and depending on the brewery's scale or sustainability efforts, anywhere from two to 10 pints of water is used to produce a single pint of beer. As our focus here is on flavour, we won't go into this further, but it's an important sustainability consideration I wanted to flag.

If the water is going to be in the finished beer, brewers refer to it as "liquor". At a minimum, the water must be of pure drinking quality, free from contaminants and contain a small amount of copper or zinc for yeast health.

INTRODUCTION:
HOPS

Hop plants are tall climbing bines that produce small cones with delicate leaves surrounding a resinous core. And it's inside this resinous core where hops' aromatic essential oils and bittering alpha acids can be found.

Often called the spice of beer, hops help contribute to beer's aroma and flavour. But they also play a few other key roles – namely providing bitterness, helping to support beer's foam, or head, formation, and preventing beer from spoiling by inhibiting the growth of bacteria.

When and how hops are used in the brew helps to determine their impact.

Hops' bittering component, alpha acids, needs to be boiled to impart bitterness. The boil brings about a structural change that allows the newly formed iso-alpha acids to dissolve into the beer. Measuring the dissolved iso-alpha acid content gives us a way to communicate a beer's bitterness level on a scale called IBU, or International Bitterness Units.

As hops' aroma and flavour compounds, the essential oils, are very volatile, they dissipate quickly during the boil. To focus on this aspect of hops' character – the "spice" – hops will be added late in the boil, just after the boil or at a time when the liquid has cooled completely, after fermentation. This final option, called dry-hopping, brings out intense

aroma and flavour, but it can make the beer taste slightly more astringent or tannic from grassy notes in the hops.

Some hops, known as bittering hops, are used primarily for their high alpha acid content, while others, called aroma hops, are prized for their essential oils. Dual-purpose hops bring the best of both.

Hops can be added to a brew in a variety of formats, from whole cones and pellets to hop extracts and oils. Whole cone hops are most traditional: the hops are harvested, dried and packaged into big bales. Pelletized hops have been ground and compressed, so they save on storage space. Finally, extracts or oils have no hop material; they are shelf-stable (and even more space-saving) liquids that impart hop bitterness, flavour and aroma.

Where hops are grown can have a significant influence on the aromas and flavours they express.

Hops require a certain amount of sunlight per day, so they tend to grow best in specific climates between the 35th and 55th parallel. This narrow latitude band includes the noted hop-growing regions of Germany, the Czech Republic, the UK and the Pacific Northwest in the USA, along with Australia and New Zealand in the southern hemisphere.

Even within each of these regions, however, hops develop unique aroma and flavour profiles influenced by the soil type, the amount of rainfall, the climate and more.

Here's an idea of how hop traits vary by region:

- German and Czech hops, including those known as noble hops, are described as being floral, spicy and perfumy

- UK-grown hops have minty, peppery and woodsy aromas

- US and new world hops from Australia and New Zealand can burst with aromas and flavours of tropical fruit, resin and pine

Hop choice can have a big impact on a beer's flavour profile. Historically, brewers would have been limited to the hops that grew locally, as they were with all other ingredients, hence why certain hop profiles are considered characteristic for certain beer styles. (You'll discover all about how hops made history in Chapter Four.)

INTRODUCTION:
YEAST

Yeast is a single-celled microorganism that's a member of the fungus family. Its scientific name, *Saccharomyces*, translates roughly to "sugar fungus".

Fermentation, broadly speaking, can encompass a range of reactions. But the one we're most interested in when it comes to brewing is yeast's conversion of sugar into alcohol and carbon dioxide, the booze and bubbles in our beer. (Hopefully the name sugar fungus makes a bit more sense now!). The reaction can also produce a whole host of other compounds, dependent on yeast strain, that impart characteristic aromas and flavours too.

There are two main species used in brewing today – ale yeast and lager yeast.

Ale yeast, more commonly known as brewer's yeast (and more technically known as *Saccharomyces cerevisiae*) also plays a role in baking, bread making and winemaking. It's thought to have been the primary yeast used in brewing for many millennia.

This species of yeast ferments at warm temperatures, approximately 16–20°C (60–72°F), which makes sense, as refrigeration wasn't widespread until the late 19th century. Ale yeast ferments rather quickly, taking only three to five days. In addition to alcohol and carbon dioxide, ale yeast also produces

compounds called esters and phenols, which give fruity or spicy notes to beer. There are over 1,500 different strains of ale yeast, each varying in their ester and phenol profiles and other fermentation characteristics.

Lager yeast (known as *Saccharomyces pastorianus*) functions at colder temperatures than ale yeast (approximately 7–13°C, 45–55°F). Additionally, the fermentation process takes much longer, often 7 to 14 days at a minimum, followed by a further few weeks or months of conditioning.

This species of yeast was better suited to the conditions of the cellars and cold caves in Bavaria where beer was being stored, or lagered, for an extended period of time in an effort to prevent spoilage. At these cold temperatures, there is minimal ester and phenol production by lager yeast, hence why lagers are said to have a "cleaner" fermentation profile than ales. (There's no fruit or spice here.) There is also less diversity amongst different lager yeast strains.

Before we could understand or isolate individual yeast strains, all beer would have been brewed with a mixed culture – and we're not just talking ale and lager yeast. Wild yeast and bacteria played their part, too. (Essentially because there was no way to avoid them.)

Environmental conditions would largely determine which microbe did the majority of the work. At room temperature, ale yeast would fare best. As the temperatures warmed up a bit, however, wild yeast and bacteria would take over, which is why beer would spoil and sour so quickly during summer. In cooler temperatures, found in the cold caves and cellars in Bavaria, for example, lager yeast would kick into gear, while ale yeast and bacteria were slowed into hibernation.

By reusing yeast from batch to batch, brewers were selecting the strains that fared best in each different environment, shaping the characteristics of ale and lager yeast over the centuries. This process of selective pressure is why certain yeast strains are now considered characteristic for certain beer styles.

With all that we now know about microbiology and refrigeration, you'd think we'd never have to see another sour beer again. But these days, there are still breweries that welcome wild microbes into their brews because of the layers of complexity they lend.

Here are a few examples of the different wild yeast and bacteria to be familiar with:

- *Brettanomyces* – previously we were talking about a sugar fungus, but this species is better known as "British fungus" as it was discovered to be the cause of the complex, "funky" flavours found in long-aged British beers. These days, "Brett" can be found in Belgian styles like lambic, *gueuze* and *saison*.

- *Lactobacillus* – this strain of bacteria produces lactic acid, a sharp, tangy acidity you may be familiar with from Greek yogurt. It's found in Berliner *weisse*, *gose* and *gueuze*, styles you'll learn more about in Chapters Five and Six.

- *Pediococcus* – this bacterium also produces lactic acid and often helps contribute to the flavour profile of styles like lambic and *gueuze*.

- *Acetobacter* – another bacterium, this strain produces acetic acid, also known as vinegar, which adds a unique sharp edge to styles like the Flanders red.

As with ale and lager yeast, we've also isolated individual wild yeast and bacteria strains to brew with, allowing modern brewers to reimagine traditional methods of fermentation. But, as you'll learn, some brewers still use those traditional methods, not only giving us an understanding of how far beer has come, but also a taste of beer's history.

THE BREWING
PROCESS

The process of turning malt, water, hops and yeast into beer does involve quite a few steps, but we'll talk through each one and its impact on a beer's finished flavour.

Brewing begins with mashing: malt, our partially germinated barley, needs to be milled or crushed (this exposes more surface area for the enzymes to act on) and mixed with water, or more accurately, liquor. During the mash, the enzymes in the crushed grains convert the starches they contain into simple sugars. This sugar is "extracted" from the malt and dissolves into the water in which the reaction is taking place.

From here, all we want to move forward with is the sugary liquid; we don't need the grains any longer as they've given up their sugars. So we separate the liquid from the solid in a process called lautering and the sweet liquid, or wort in brewing terms, moves on to the next step – the boil.

During the boil is when we add our hops. The compounds in hops that make beer bitter, the alpha acids, need to be boiled in order to change shape, dissolve into the liquid and impart their bitterness. The boil also helps to clarify the beer, making any proteins settle out. And importantly, it's a sanitation step. The high temperatures can also cause some caramelization of the sugars in

the malt, making malt's flavours even more rich.

From here on out, sanitation is key. The boiled, bittersweet wort must be filtered to remove any hop debris and cooled to bring it down to a suitable fermentation temperature, which depends on whether it's being fermented with ale or lager yeast.

The beer is then given time to ferment. Yeast is "pitched" (ie. added to the wort) and as the yeast replicates, the sugar in the solution is consumed and alcohol and carbon dioxide are produced, along with esters and phenols (the concentration of which is dependent upon the yeast strain being used).

Fermentation is a pretty wild process and there are often lots of other compounds that are produced that yeast will go back in and clean up – this is called the conditioning phase. As the beer matures, any rough flavours age out. Lagers condition for longer than ales, further enhancing their "clean" fermentation character. After conditioning, the yeast will be recovered so it can be reused, or re-pitched, as this helps with consistency from batch to batch.

Beer will typically brighten, or clarify, during the conditioning phase, as yeast and other particulates settle out. Depending on the brewery size or style of beer, further steps may be taken to improve beer's brightness and shelf-stability. Filtration is often used to remove particulates and increase clarity, while pasteurization, briefly heating the beer to kill all remaining microorganisms, gives the beer a longer shelf life. Alternatively, beers can remain unfiltered and unpasteurized.

From here, the beer is packaged – in kegs, bottles, cans or casks – and shipped out to consumers to enjoy.

This is our modern brewing process. As you'll learn, it has changed significantly over the years.

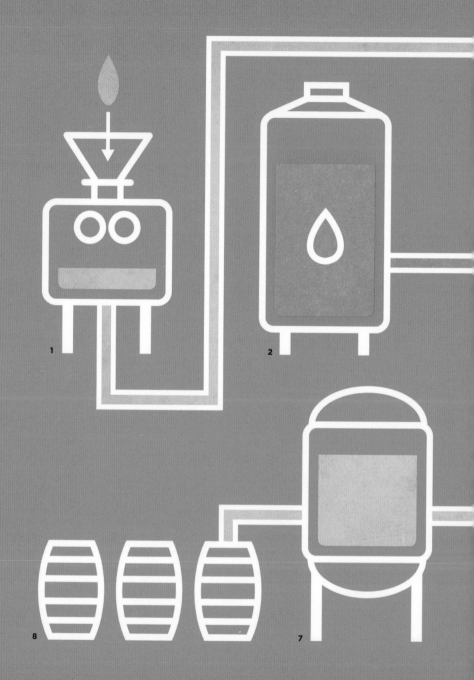

1. MILLING (MALT ADDED)   2. (WATER ADDED)   3. MASHING AND LAUTERING   4. BOILING (HOPS ADDED)

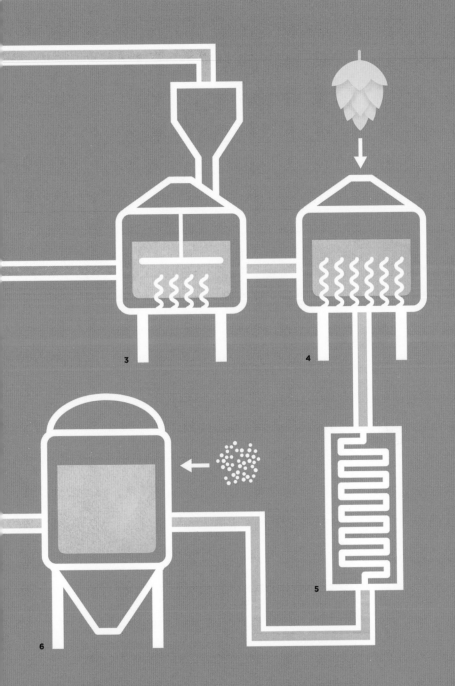

3

4

5

6

5. COOLING 6. FERMENTATION (YEAST ADDED) 7. CONDITIONING 8. PACKAGING

A BRIEF SKIM OF BEER HISTORY:
ANCIENT TIMES TO THE INDUSTRIAL AGE

Wheat and barley are thought to have been domesticated around 10,000 years ago, closely tied to the origins of agriculture.

After the domestication of grains, we see the first archaeological evidence of beer (or more broadly "grain-based fermented beverages") dating back to 7000 BCE from China (using rice), followed by Mesopotamia and Egypt (brewed with wheat or barley). By 4000 BCE, we've got pictorial evidence of brewing. Then by 2500 BCE we know the Sumerians, the first great civilization of the ancient Middle East, were not only brewing, but brewing a range of beers.

The brewing process back then likely wouldn't look very similar to the process today, however.

A text from early Mesopotamian cultures called the Hymn to Ninkasi details the brewing process from around 1800 BCE. It suggests beer was brewed with cakes made of malted barley called bappir, which is often translated as "beer bread". The grains would be soaked, sprouted and air- or sun-dried, then ground and clumped together into cakes, which may even have been baked. These cakes were then dissolved into jars of warm water, allowing for the mashing process to begin the conversion of starches to sugars.

A variety of herbs or spices could have been incorporated (this is all pre-hops), and it's likely grapes or raisins may have been included to introduce yeast and get fermentation going (as one of yeast's natural habitats is on the skin of fruits). The beer would need to be consumed rather quickly as it was susceptible to spoilage.

Beer was typically produced on a domestic scale and was both brewed and served by women. Many ancient cultures even had female goddesses they'd worship who they thought were responsible for the success of the brew.

Women remained involved in brewing up through the Middle Ages and beyond. They became known as brewsters or alewives and they brewed and served a range of beers of varying strengths on estates, in taverns and at inns. All members of society would consume the lowest-strength beers, as beer was safer than water then because of the boil, and provided some nutrients, too. These brown, smoky, slightly sour, low alcohol beers certainly weren't the beers that were going to build an industry, however.

As the church and state got involved, brewing became more organized. Self-sufficiency, an important tenet of monastic life, led to the building of abbey breweries, giving us the first large-scale production of beer in medieval Europe in the 8th and 9th centuries. Official state breweries followed, as beer became a lucrative source of revenue. By the 11th and 12th centuries, brewing began to flourish in cities and within a few hundred years brewers' guilds were established from London to Munich.

Soon brewing became a more professional – and more profitable – pursuit. By the 1500s, producing beer and selling beer became two separate activities, with brewing largely taken over by men. Commercial breweries in cities began selling into taverns at this time, but the practice didn't really take off until they could scale. And the Industrial Revolution allowed them to do just that, largely making small-scale brewing a thing of the past.

Beginning in the 1700s, changes began to take place that helped build our scientific understanding of brewing, which laid the foundation for expansion and helped build our modern beer industry.

From here on out, you'll learn how technology, trade, taste preferences and more have created and shaped the beers we know and love today.

WHAT WE MEAN BY
BEER STYLES

Before we start our story, I've got to say a few words on styles. The aim of this book is to help you taste your way through the evolution of beer styles over time, hopefully giving you an understanding of how different beer styles have influenced each other, what sets each style apart, and how we got to our modern-day boom time for beer.

So what is a beer style? There are several different definitions, but I see style guidelines as a set of characteristics that help people wrap their heads around beer. They allow the brewer to tell the drinker what to expect from a beer in terms of colour, aroma, flavour, body and strength.

The term "beer style" was first used by the late British beer writer Michael Jackson in 1977 in his *World Guide to Beer*. Previous terms had been used to group similar beers, from "kinds" to "varieties" to "types", but using the word styles in this context was new.

Nearly a decade later, the idea of grouping beers by similar production methods, ingredients or flavours got adopted by homebrewers in the US who were looking to categorize and classify the beers they brewed for competitions.

The Beer Judge Certification Program (BJCP) first introduced its *Style Guidelines* in 1997 and has revised them every few

years since. These are largely seen as the reference for beer styles today.

Not only are they used in judging home brewing competitions, they're also used for studying for beer certifications offered through the Cicerone® Certification Program. As these are the style guidelines I'm familiar with from my studies, and as I'd like for this book to serve as a helpful reference for others who choose to pursue various levels of their Cicerone® certification, I've decided to use the BCJP guidelines as the framework for this book.

That said, in the USA the Brewers' Association (BA) also provides style guidelines. These are reviewed and revised yearly. While that makes the BA guidelines more difficult to study from, as they are continually changing, they're very helpful for tracking trends and seeing when new beer styles are officially recognized for judging in competitions, primarily the Great American Beer Festival. For example, the "Imperial or Double India Pale Ale" was first introduced as a category in 2003, while "Juicy or Hazy India Pale Ale" was a much more recent introduction in 2018.

As they're simply guidelines, not every beer fits a style and not every brewer brews to style – in fact, some brewers actively push the boundaries, sometimes developing new styles in the process.

And as you're about to learn, styles change over time. Some styles evolved in certain places because of the ingredients or equipment available there, but as new ingredients became available or as our understanding of the brewing process improved, the styles evolved, again. Other factors like technology, changing consumer preference, international influence, regulations, war and more have all had an impact.

I think Randy Mosher, author of *Tasting Beer*, says it best: "Styles honour the past and give order to the present."

So let's go explore beer's evolution, one sip at a time.

Two last notes: If a specific beer is said to have spurred the development of a certain style, that beer has been selected as the story to tell and beer to taste, regardless of the brewery's current ownership.

Additionally, while I couldn't fit every style into this book, I've done my best to tie related styles together so you understand their relationships. There are plenty more great books that dive far deeper into these beer styles, which you can find mentioned in the conclusion.

•CHAPTER• ONE • 1

1600s–1870s

FROM SMOKY BROWN BEER TO GOLDEN LAGER, MALT MODERNIZES

Barley needs to be malted in order to give brewers access to the starchy energy reserves inside each kernel (which, in turn, provide the sugars yeast needs for fermentation).

In the final step of the malting process, germination is halted in its tracks by the application of heat to dry, then toast the grains. But drying the grains wasn't all that easy centuries ago.

Historically, malt was either air-dried or dried over a crackling wood fire, meaning much of the malt used for brewing was either rather flavourless (as most of malt's flavour comes from the heat of the kilning process) or an uneven colour and full of smoke (it's tough to control those flames and even tougher to control the smoke!).

In Britain, around the turn of the 18th century, new fuel sources and kilning methods were developed. Over time, maltsters in Britain and beyond had enough control over kilning to produce smoke-free, black, amber and truly golden-coloured malt. And with that, introduce a whole new range of beer colours, flavours and styles.

It's worth mentioning early here that there wasn't actually a standardized scale for measuring beer colour until 1883. The Lovibond Scale was created by Joseph Lovibond after taking inspiration from the colourful stained-glass windows at Salisbury Cathedral.

So while the colours and colour changes we'll be discussing in Chapter One couldn't be measured in the way we measure beer colour today, these tales are recounted time and time again in beer history books explaining how we reached the pinnacle that is pilsner malt.

As there wasn't a scale, it's also important to note the colour descriptors themselves are relative – what I may call amber, you might call copper. But we do know pale malt was paler than brown malt and that pilsner malt gave the golden hue everyone was gunning for.

Curious how it all happened and what beer styles these changes helped create along the way? Read on.

SMOKY AND BROWN
1600s

As brewers in Britain were not quite fortunate enough, climate-wise, to air-dry malt, most malts produced there were dried via the only viable alternative – over a crackling wood fire.

Directly fired over an open flame, most kilned malt produced up through the 1600s had an uneven colour and a smoky aroma and flavour.

By the 1700s, improvements had been made to malting technology that enabled the use of indirect heat and alternative fuel sources, meaning malt no longer had to taste smoky. And from then on, most breweries never looked back.

But a few breweries in the storied town of Bamberg, Germany kept up the smoke beer tradition. Which conveniently gives us a taste of history.

Rauchbier, or 'smoke beer' in German, is typically defined as a *Märzen* (a malty, amber coloured German lager) brewed with beechwood-smoked malt. But all different kinds of wood can and have been used for malt kilning in the past, from oak and maple, to applewood and more.

Although modern *Rauchbier* is amber in colour, historically, wood-dried malts would likely have given beer a darker brown hue. (You'll learn how we've improved our kilning capabilities shortly!)

For an idea of what many beers might have tasted like 400 years ago, try the *Märzen* from Bamberg's own Schlenkerla brewery. Known for its aromas of smoky bacon or barbeque sauce, I will caution you the first sip is always a surprise, but hang in there for the second and see if it grows on you.

Smoke beer not for you? You're in luck – most brewers agreed and shifted away from smoked malts as quickly as they could. Here's what came next.

TASTE THIS SCHLENKERLA MÄRZEN	FLAVOUR SMOKY BACON, BBQ	ABV 5.1%
(STYLE) RAUCHBIER		
ORIGIN BAMBERG, GERMANY	**NOTES** WHILE MANY BREWERIES WERE QUICK TO MOVE AWAY FROM SMOKED MALTS IN THE EARLY 1700S, SCHLENKERLA HAS BECOME RENOWNED FOR THEIR USE. FOR THE ULTIMATE EXPERIENCE, TREK TO BAMBERG AND TRY THIS ON TAP. IT TRULY IS A TASTE OF HISTORY. TOO SMOKY FOR YOU? HEAD OVER TO SPEZIAL ACROSS TOWN – THEY SERVE A SMOKED RADLER! HALF SMOKED BEER, HALF LEMONADE AND WHOLLY INTRIGUING.	

LESS SMOKY, BUT STILL BROWN
1700s, in the city

As British maltsters moved away from open flames to indirect heat, they left behind the smoky flavours of the past.

But kilning was still a rather imprecise science. Not enough heat and your malt wouldn't dry, meaning the malt would mould or the barley kernel would continue its germination and you'd lose those all-important sugars to a new plant. Too much heat, however, and the grains could catch fire and combust. So you'd be left without any sugar that way too.

As it was problematic to apply too little or too much heat, most malt was kilned somewhere in between, taking on a basic shade of brown. This brown malt, primarily produced in Hertfordshire, became particularly popular with London breweries at the turn of the 18th century. Large quantities were being used to produce dark brown, sweet, heavy ales.

At this time, the Industrial Revolution was beginning, enabling breweries to scale to meet the demands of London's growing and thirsty population.

A stronger, more hopped version of the heavy, sweet brown beer soon developed. Popular with the city's river and ticket porters, workers employed to unload ships or carry goods across the city, the beer style took on their name in the 1720s – porter.

Around the turn of the century when malts were still slightly smoky, the beer would be aged for a few months to let some of the smoke character from the wood-fired malt mellow out.

Even as malt quality improved, however, this aging practice continued and extended.

Large vats of older "stale" beer would be aged for up to two years, then blended with younger "running" or "mild" beer before serving. The older beer would contribute a mature flavour, while the younger beer provided a bit of carbonation.

(Although no longer practised in England, this method of aging and blending had an unexpected influence on Belgian brewing, which we'll discuss in Chapter Five).

If sweet and heavy doesn't sound like a porter to you, that's because the style has changed considerably over its nearly 300-year-old history.

As you'll learn, brewers quickly moved away from using large quantities of brown malts when reliably produced pale malts came on the scene.

In the late 1700s, a new bit of brewing technology – the hydrometer – changed brewing forever. It helped brewers understand how much sugar was actually being extracted from the malt they were brewing with. And, spoiler alert, brown malt wasn't all that efficient when it came to extracting sugars for the brew.

Prolonged exposure to high temperatures kills off malt's enzymes, meaning the darker the malt, the less fermentable sugar it can contribute, or in brewing terms, the lower the extract. Most of brown malt's sugars were too complex to be fermented by yeast so they'd remain in the finished beer, increasing the beer's perceived sweetness, flavour and body.

Armed with this knowledge, brewers knew it would be much more efficient to use more pale malts than dark, adding in only a small quantity of dark malts for colour and flavour. Porter soon became drier, or less sweet, as pale malts provided sugars that could be fully fermented by yeast.

So this early sweet, heavy iteration of porter was largely forgotten about. But I've got a tasting recommendation for you that's reminiscent of porter's past – a sweet stout.

Sweet stouts, also known as milk stouts, first developed in England in the early 1900s. They're dark brown in colour from the use of dark malts, but they've got a sweetness and heaviness to them, not from the malt, but from an additional ingredient called lactose, or milk sugar.

While yeast ferments most simple sugars into alcohol and carbon dioxide, there are certain sugars it can't process, and lactose is one of them.

This means if lactose is added into a brew it won't be fermented by yeast and will instead remain in the finished beer. Lactose adds sweetness and a bit of body, too, making the beer feel heavier on your tongue. Dark, sweet, heavy – get it?

While not exactly traditional, this is one way to re-imagine what an early 18th century porter may have tasted like. Because when a new type of malt was introduced the following century, the flavour of porter changed forever.

TASTE THIS LEFT HAND MILK STOUT	FLAVOUR MILK CHOCOLATE, COFFEE AND CREAM	ABV 6%
(STYLE) SWEET STOUT		
ORIGIN LONGMONT, COLORADO, USA	**NOTES** WHILE THE EARLIEST ITERATION OF PORTER ISN'T ACTUALLY BREWED ANY MORE, THE MODERN DAY SWEET OR MILK STOUT HAS SIMILAR FLAVOURS THAT CAN GIVE US A TASTE OF HISTORY.	

LIGHTENING UP
1700s, in the country

Kilning continued to improve with the introduction of a new fuel source: the discovery of how to produce coke from coal.

Coal was considered unsuitable for use in malting because it produced sulphurs, tars and smoky compounds. Heat it to extreme temperatures though and those combustibles are driven off, producing coke. Coke allowed for far greater temperature control, not only producing a paler shade of malt, but a cleaner, more consistent flavour too.

Initially though, quantities were limited, and prices were high. (The fact pale malts were much more efficient and had a higher extract *kept* prices high too.) Effectively, these malts were all but out of reach for city breweries producing on an industrial scale.

Estate brewers on country manors were brewing on a much smaller scale than those in the city, however. So although pale malts were expensive, they weren't out of reach for use in small batches These early pale, or amber-coloured, malts were put to use in several different styles on the manor.

One single batch of malt would be used for multiple mashes. The first lot of liquid drawn off from the malt would have the most sugar and produce the strongest wort. More hot water would then be added to the grains, extracting any remaining sugar and producing a slightly weaker wort. This process was repeated two or three times.

In this practice, referred to as parti-gyle brewing, the different worts (or "gyles") would be blended to produce beers of varying strengths. October beer and ale were the strongest, followed by stock ale (which was brewed for aging), and finally, table and small beers, brewed to consume fresh.

By the 1700s, it was understood that hops and high alcohol both acted as preservatives, so as the strength declined with the table and small beers, they were given a higher charge of hops to keep them from going off.

(It's worth noting in England at this time, beer and ale were two separate beverages: "beer" was hopped, while "ale" wasn't. We'll explore this distinction more in Chapter Four, but it eventually disappeared by the 1800s. By then, nearly all ales had some quantity of hops for preservation. Going forward, I'll refer to both October brews as October ales, for convenience.)

The most prized brew on the manor was of course the strong October ale. As brewing was still a seasonal activity, prior to the advent of refrigeration in the late 1800s, brewing used to take

>>

place October through March or April only. Brewed in autumn with freshly harvested malt and hops, October ales were strong enough to age at least one year, sometimes two, before being consumed.

The pale malts go through a long boil to give the beer its deep amber hue. Incredibly rich and complex, there's a toffee-like sweetness from the malt and sherry notes from the beer's high alcohol content and long aging period.

The modern beer that's considered to be today's best representation of a traditional October ale is J W Lee's Harvest Ale (despite only being brewed since 1986!).

As in the past, it's brewed with 100% British pale ale malts (in this case the Maris Otter varietal), and 100% British hops (specifically East Kent Goldings, which you'll read more about in Chapter

Four.) It's only brewed once a year in October after – you guessed it – harvest.

As I realize this book can be enjoyed year round, not just during the traditional brewing season, this particular beer might be a bit tough to find. If you get stuck, the next best thing would be a barley wine (skip ahead to Chapter Two for a sneak peek about that style).

While traditional October ales are hard to find these days, they've had a huge influence on some of today's most popular styles. But beers got a bit darker before brewers saw the light.

TASTE THIS J W LEE'S HARVEST ALE	FLAVOUR TOFFEE, SHERRY, RICH	ABV 11.5%
(STYLE) OCTOBER ALE*		
ORIGIN MANCHESTER, ENGLAND	**NOTES** BREWED ONCE A YEAR AND VINTAGE DATED, EACH BATCH IS UNIQUE. WITH A LONG AGING PERIOD, NEW FLAVOURS DEVELOP, GIVING A RICHNESS AND DEPTH TO THE BEER – SOME MIGHT SAY IT'S ALMOST WINE-LIKE!	

*AS OCTOBER ALE IS A HISTORICAL BEER, IT IS NOT LISTED AS A STYLE IN ANY CURRENT STYLE GUIDELINES. BJCP INCLUDES J W LEE'S HARVEST ALE AS AN EXAMPLE OF AN ENGLISH BARLEYWINE, SO THAT WOULD BE THE CLOSEST MODERN-DAY FIT.

DARKENING TO NIGHT
1817

As the various pale ales from the countryside started making their way into the city, porter drinkers began to take notice.

Not only was this beer lighter in colour, it was also lighter in flavour. Not sweet, heavy and dark, but drier and crisper. (Manorial breweries couldn't just afford the best quality pale malts, they also sourced the best available hops. Hops contribute bitterness to beer, which helps to balance out malt's sweetness and give the beer a refreshing edge.)

Consumers developed a taste for these hoppier amber-coloured beers conveniently when the hydrometer shone a light on the inefficiencies of brewing with all brown malt, around the 1780s. This was also shortly after the thermometer began to be used by brewers (its first documented use in brewing was in 1758). Instead of relying on empirical methods, temperature could be measured and, more importantly, controlled.

This meant pale malts could be produced with much more precision and in much higher quantities. Soon the dark brown porter beer began to lighten in body and lose some of its colour and roasted flavour.

So how did brewers keep the colour and flavour consumers were used to?

They used all kinds of concoctions – but mainly the addition of burned or caramelized sugars (even if they weren't strictly legal).

That all changed, however, in 1817 when Daniel Wheeler applied for a patent for a drum roaster. Applying coffee roasting techniques to malting, the malt would be exposed to temperatures of 200°C (400°F) or more.

For any homebrewers out there who have ever brewed with black patent malt – Wheeler's patent is where the name comes from*. (Pretty cool, huh?)

Although the name porter was first used in the 1720s, and the dark brown beer style it described had been around for decades prior, the beer we know as porter changed forever because of Wheeler's invention of black malt.

With a primarily pale malt base and a handful of black malt for colour and flavour, the beer would become much lighter in body and darker in colour with more roast, burned notes. Is this starting to sound a bit more similar to the porters you're familiar with?

Interestingly, English porters today are described as having a restrained roasted flavour without any burned notes. As we're aiming for a taste of history – and you can bet that black malt was harsh

>>

– I've recommended an American-style porter, as they're often sharper with a lightly burned character.

As if its 300-year history isn't multifaceted enough, the style has continued to change and evolve. It even gave rise to stout (initially known as a stout porter) and several other spinoffs.

Continue exploring these styles in the call-out box.

* Interestingly, Wheeler's patent was overturned in 1819 when a challenge was brought that his invention was no different from common coffee roasters that had been used for a century prior. But by then, the name "patent malt" had stuck.

TASTE THIS ANCHOR PORTER	FLAVOUR DARK CHOCOLATE, COFFEE, LIQUORICE	ABV 5.6%
(STYLE) AMERICAN PORTER	**NOTES** WHILE PORTER ORIGINATED IN ENGLAND, MOST MODERN ENGLISH PORTERS ARE NO LONGER BREWED WITH BLACK PATENT MALT. THIS AMERICAN EXAMPLE FROM ANCHOR IS, GIVING IT NOTES OF ROASTED COFFEE AND BURNED TOAST.	
ORIGIN SAN FRANCISCO, CALIFORNIA, USA		

A LITTLE MORE
TO SAY ON PORTER AND STOUT...

Porter and stout are tricky styles to define these days. Why, you ask?

Primarily because both styles have changed significantly since first brewed. Whether it's because of new technology, new ingredients or changing consumer preference, the beers we drink today called porters are nothing like their historical relatives from 300 years ago.

How did stout get caught up in this mess? Stout was initially named a "stouter kind of porter", for its more "stout" body and strength, so the two are inherently tied together.

Here's a simple breakdown of what (most) people agree to be the difference between a porter and a stout, along with a few more tasting recommendations.

English porter, simply called porter in the UK, should taste smooth with rich chocolate and caramel flavours. It shouldn't be overly roasty and definitely shouldn't taste burned. That's because most porters don't actually use black malts these days; often the darkest malts used are brown or chocolate malts.

Stouts aren't necessarily stronger than porters, alcohol-wise, anymore, but their flavours are certainly more robust.

All stouts will have roasted, coffee-like notes from the use of black malt. That said, there's a broad range of flavours across stouts' various sub-styles – from Irish (like Guinness), to oatmeal and Imperial.

Irish stout, sometimes called Irish dry stout, uses a small amount of roasted un-malted barley in the brew. These grains are a bit astringent, or tannic, so they leave a drying sensation in your mouth after each sip. You might be thinking: but the Guinness I've had is full and creamy? It only tastes that way on draught because of the type of gas used to dispense it. Guinness uses nitrogen which makes loads of tiny bubbles in the beer, giving it a smooth, creamy character. Try it from a bottle though and it will taste thinner with a more astringent, almost burned, bite.

Oatmeal stouts on the other hand are full and smooth as the oats add a bit more body to the beer, making it feel nice and creamy. They can also give the beer a mild nutty, grainy, or earthy flavour too.

Imperial stouts pack a punch. Back in the 1700s, English porters, along with other styles, started making their way to Russia. Initially exported from Burton upon Trent in the English Midlands, Russia introduced high tariffs on English imports to help stimulate their own industry. Realizing they couldn't produce porter quite as well as the Brits could though, tariffs were removed on porter in particular and London brewers picked up where Burton left off.

The strongest stout porter from London's Barclay Perkins Brewery was a favourite of the Russian Imperial Court, hence the style's later name Imperial stout.

TASTE THIS FULLER'S LONDON PORTER (STYLE) ENGLISH PORTER ORIGIN LONDON, ENGLAND	FLAVOUR CHOCOLATE, CARAMEL	ABV 5.4%
	NOTES THIS STYLE HAS CHANGED A LOT OVER THE YEARS, DECLINING IN POPULARITY AND EVENTUALLY DISAPPEARING IN THE 1950S. REDISCOVERED IN THE 1970S WITH THE CRAFT BEER MOVEMENT, FULLER'S LONDON PORTER IS CONSIDERED THE MODERN CLASSIC.	

TASTE THIS GUINNESS ORIGINAL (STYLE) IRISH STOUT ORIGIN DUBLIN, IRELAND	FLAVOUR BITTERSWEET, ROASTED COFFEE	ABV 5%
	NOTES THE ORIGINAL "STOUTER KIND OF PORTER." AFTER WORLD WAR II, GUINNESS BEGAN USING ROASTED UN-MALTED BARLEY, WHICH GIVES THIS BEER ITS DARK CHOCOLATE AND COFFEE CHARACTER, ALONG WITH A TOUCH OF DRYNESS OR ASTRINGENCY IN THE FINISH.	

TASTE THIS NORTH COAST OLD RASPUTIN (STYLE) IMPERIAL STOUT ORIGIN FORT BRAGG, CALIFORNIA, USA	FLAVOUR RICH, FULL BODIED, NOTES OF COFFEE, DARK CHOCOLATE, AND DRIED FRUIT	ABV 9%
	NOTES YOU MAY SEE THIS STYLE CALLED RUSSIAN IMPERIAL STOUT, AS THE RUSSIAN IMPERIAL COURT WERE KNOWN FANS. THE STRENGTH OF THIS STYLE MAKES THIS BEER RICH, COMPLEX AND QUITE INTENSE. VERY POPULAR WITH MODERN DAY CRAFT BREWERIES.	

PALE PROVES POPULAR
1829

With its colonies around the world needing goods, Britain became an exporting nation, and beer was no exception. Beer shipments to the American colonies began in the late 1600s, but it's the exports to India in the 1700s that we're interested in here.

The East India Company was the main supplier between Britain and the colonies in India at this time. While they were bringing back rarities from India to sell back home for a pretty penny, the ships' captains loaded up the boats with consumer goods for the outbound journey.

Nearby the East India Company docks was Bow Brewery, founded in 1752 and run by George Hodgson, he supplied both porter and strong October ale to the East Indiamen.

By the 1760s, it was well understood that hops helped to preserve beer. Additionally, it has been documented that beers of all strengths and styles – from small beer and table beer, to porter – were sent to India as early as the 1700s.

So while there are many myths that a strong, highly hopped beer was invented in London specifically for the journey to India, there isn't much evidence to support the claim. The beer Hodgson shipped was likely very similar to the

strong, long-aged October ales already being brewed at the time, but it may have been more highly hopped for preservation.

So where did the name "India Pale Ale" actually come from? Historical records show the name was first used in print in an 1829 newspaper advertisement in Australia – only after the style began being brewed in Burton upon Trent in the English Midlands.

Beer exports weren't only being shipped from London. Brewers in Burton had a long history of exporting ales to Russia and the Baltics, starting in the mid-1700s. (Known primarily for the strong, dark, sweet and heavy Burton ale, this beer eventually evolved into the barleywine style once Burton brewers took up the IPA mantle.)

In the late 1760s, Burton breweries had a formal treaty with Catherine the Great, but in 1783, Russia imposed a steep tax on imports to stimulate the Russian industry instead. Things went from bad to worse with the Napoleonic wars and further tariffs. By the 1820s, Burton's brewing output was significantly less than it had been decades prior.

While London's Bow Brewery was certainly the best-known brewer of pale ales and beers destined for India, Hodgson gained his reputation not

>>

only because of the quality and consistency of his products, but because of his rather ruthless business practices. They caught up with him, however, and eventually the brewery's monopoly on the market ended around 1820.

Conveniently, Burton had capacity to brew and the East India Company were after new suppliers. So the company director visited Samuel Allsopp, of the Allsopp Brewery in Burton, with a bottle of beer from Bow Brewery and asked him to produce a similar beer for export to India.

Initially, the beer was too dark, too sweet, too strong and in need of more aging time and more bitterness. The recipe was re-tooled, and by 1826, Allsopp's beer was selling for the same price as Hodgson's.

What made the difference? Two key factors, the malt and the water.

The maltsters at Allsopp produced what they called extra pale or white malt, which was produced at lower kilning temperatures and gave the finished beer a deep gold to light amber colour.

There was also something in the water. Burton's local wells contained a mineral called gypsum, which made the beer even paler because less colour was extracted from the malt. (Gypsum

also made the beer drier, more bitter and improved the beer's clarity and consistency. But we'll discuss that in more detail in Chapter Three.)

By the 1830s, Burton had become the place to brew IPA. And by mid-century, IPA was no longer just for export – it became popular at home. Railways allowed for distribution across the country and production rates increased by 50% within one year.

While there's no evidence the initial beers that Bow Brewery produced for India were any different than the strong, aged pale ales of the time, it's noted that IPA brewed for home consumption was less strong and less bitter but was still aged prior to serving.

Bright amber in colour, this dry, bitter beer was a real thirst quencher. Compared to a porter, IPA was more crisp, clean, and refreshing. No dark malts meant no roasted notes. Just a pale, biscuity malt base, loaded up with hop bitterness.

You'll notice I've recommended an "English IPA" style. What does that mean exactly?

We'll discuss the hops used in IPA and how they've changed over the years in more detail in Chapter Four. But for now, all you need to know is most modern IPAs available today are brewed in an American-style, meaning with punchy, citrusy, resiny American hops.

As our goal here is to have a taste of history (and the aforementioned hops weren't around in the mid-1800s), we're going with something closer to what would have been: an English IPA brewed with herbal, earthy hops and a mild bitterness. English IPAs are known for being a bit more malt-forward, and as this chapter is all about the malt, it's a perfect fit.

By the mid-19th century, pale ales and IPAs had replaced porter as the most popular beer in England. And, as England was a global superpower at the time, other countries began to take notice. Brewers from other countries headed to England to see what they could learn about these new pale malting techniques.

Soon, pale malts began to prove popular worldwide.

TASTE THIS WORTHINGTON'S WHITE SHIELD	**FLAVOUR** WOODY, SPICY HOPS, BISCUITY MALT BODY, TOUCH OF FRUIT, BITTER	**ABV** 5.6%
(STYLE) ENGLISH IPA	**NOTES** ONE OF THE LAST SURVIVING EXAMPLES OF THE HISTORICAL BURTON IPA, WORTHINGTON'S WHITE SHIELD HAS BEEN BREWED BY VARIOUS OWNERS OVER THE YEARS, BUT ULTIMATELY THE RECIPE HARKENS BACK TO 1830S BURTON.	
ORIGIN BURTON UPON TRENT, ENGLAND		

CLOSER WITH COPPER
1841

As pale ales from England travelled the globe, brewers abroad took notice.

Brewers in Germany's southern region of Bavaria give rise to the family of lager beers in the 1500s (more on this in Chapter Five), but, 300 years on, their brewing techniques remained rather rudimental. Most brewers were producing smoky, dark brown lagers as indirect heat hadn't been introduced here yet. But that was about to change.

By the 1830s, German brewing began to industrialize. And in 1833, a couple of young brewers from Austria and Germany, Anton Dreher from Klein-Schwechat brewery in Vienna and Gabriel Sedlmayr from Munich's Spaten, were sent to England to learn all they could about these pale malts.

Legend has it a little industrial espionage may have taken place. You know, the classic hollow walking stick trick – allowing them to collect a sample of the fermenting beer while touring a brewery to then assess in private later on.

Who's to say what actually happened? But we do know both Dreher and Sedlmayr returned home and revolutionised their local brewing industries.

Not only were they able to produce smoke-free malts, finally ridding the

region's dark brown lagers of any smoky flavours. They also introduced paler malt than previously available, Vienna and Munich malts, respectively.

Imparting a beautiful copper hue and lightly nutty note, Dreher's Vienna malt gave rise to the aptly known, Vienna lager in 1841.

Impressive at the time, Vienna lager was quickly usurped by the golden-hued pilsners only a year later, so it lost ground at home.

It found fans on the other side of the world though – more specifically, Mexico. In the late 1800s, Austrians immigrated to Mexico and brought their local beer style with them, giving rise to beers like Modelo Negra.

Nearly a century later in America, the Vienna lager inspired Brooklyn Brewery's flagship Brooklyn Lager.

These days, neither of the aforementioned beers are actually brewed with any traditional Vienna malts, as often caramel malts (which you'll learn more about shortly) are subbed in instead.

Truthfully, traditional examples of Vienna lager are hard to find today. A few US breweries, like Devil's Backbone and Chuckanut, have one in their line-up, but in the UK they're often only one-offs or produced seasonally.

It seems this style's popularity was short-lived, as copper was just one step closer on beer's journey to gold.

Meanwhile in Germany, Sedlmayr put his Munich malts to use in 1841 to brew the first *Märzen* at Spaten.

While the name *Märzen*, or "March beer", had been around much longer and historically meant a strong beer that was brewed in March and lagered in cold caves over the summer, the use of his new Munich malt helped to shape the modern definition of the style – a German amber lager.

Compared to Vienna malts, Munich malts are a touch darker, giving the *Märzen* more of a malty richness and bready, toasty flavours. In 1872, a slightly lighter shade of *Märzen*, said to be brewed in the Viennese style, was introduced at Oktoberfest and became the standard festival beer for more than 100 years. In 1990, however, a lighter, golden Festbier was adopted. (Told you everybody wants to go for gold!)

TASTE THIS WELTENBURGER KLOSTER ANNO 1050	FLAVOUR BREADY, TOASTY, CLEAN FERMENTATION PROFILE	ABV 5.5%
(STYLE) MÄRZEN		
ORIGIN KELHEIM, GERMANY	**NOTES** A TRADITIONAL EXAMPLE OF EITHER VIENNA LAGER OR MÄRZEN CAN BE A BIT TRICKY TO FIND. MOST BEERS LABELLED OKTOBERFEST BEERS USED TO BE MÄRZENS, BUT NOW THEY'RE A LIGHTER, GOLDEN COLOUR INSTEAD. GIVE THIS TRADITIONAL GERMAN AMBER LAGER A GO TO GET A TASTE OF MUNICH MALTS AND THEIR RICH, BREADY CHARACTER.	

GOING FOR GOLD
1842

It wasn't only the German and Viennese brewers looking to the English for inspiration. So, too, did the Bohemians. Particularly, the local townspeople from Pilsen.

Pilsen had formerly been renowned for its brewing, but its beer quality took a nosedive in the 1830s, so the city officials finally did something about it. (Note, this was only after the local brewers met and dumped 36 barrels of beer they declared to be undrinkable right in the town square. Harsh.)

The townspeople invested in a brand-new brewery and the right man for the job – Bavarian brewer Josef Groll. The plan was to capitalize on the high-quality malt and hops in the region and brew a lager beer that could rival the success of England's pale ales.

Well, they didn't just rival the pale ale, they blew it out of the water.

The combination of premium local ingredients, a state-of-the-art brewery and a well-built business plan gave birth to Pilsner Urquell in 1842. Named after the city where it all began, pilsner would eventually become the most popular beer style in the world.

As you can probably tell, there's a lot to unpack here, and yes, we'll be revisiting this style again and again.

Let's stick to the theme here and home in on the hue. Pilsner was unlike any beer that had ever been seen before – it was the world's first truly golden lager.

Finally managing to fine-tune the kilning techniques that had been improving in England, Josef Groll turned the local barley into a beautiful, burnished gold malt. (In fact, it has been suggested the first batch of malt used to brew Pilsner Urquell was kilned in an English kiln in an apparent act of industrial espionage.)

Today known as pilsner malt, these lightly kilned grains give beers a slightly sweet, lightly grainy flavour.

While many modern pilsner-style lagers are lighter in colour, Pilsner Urquell is brewed using a traditional decoction mash and an extended boil. Both of these steps darken the beer's colour slightly as the sugars in the malt caramelize, creating a deeper golden hue.

During a decoction mash, a portion of the mash is removed, heated up in a separate kettle, then added back into the main mash to increase the overall temperature. This process creates a real depth of malt flavour and provides a firm foundation for the style's assertive bitterness and spicy hop character.

>>

Although hop rates are high, the bready, caramelly malt softens the bitterness and prevents it from becoming too harsh, making Pilsner Urquell both incredibly complex and incredibly refreshing.

Launched in the right place and at the right time, an eye-catching colour and a few convenient coincidences helped the style take over the world. But we'll get to that in Chapter Two.

TASTE THIS	FLAVOUR	ABV
PILSNER URQUELL	CARAMEL SWEETNESS, SPICY HOPS, ASSERTIVE BITTERNESS	4.4%
(STYLE)		
CZECH PILSNER / CZECH PREMIUM PALE LAGER		

NOTES
THIRSTY FOR MORE? DON'T YOU WORRY, THERE'S PLENTY MORE TO SAY ABOUT THE ORIGINAL GOLDEN LAGER IN CHAPTER TWO! FOR NOW, HERE'S A FUN FACT: URQUELL TRANSLATES TO "ORIGINAL" OR "ORIGINAL SOURCE". TO BEST ENJOY THE ORIGINAL PILSNER IN ALL ITS GLORY, I HIGHLY RECOMMEND A VISIT TO THE BREWERY IN PILSEN. (YOU'LL FIND THIS AND MORE OF MY TRAVEL TIPS IN THE CONCLUSION!)

ORIGIN
PILSEN, CZECH REPUBLIC

A SWEET FINISH
1870

Before we move away from malt, we've got a sweet little note to finish on.

While golden pilsner malt has arguably had the biggest influence on beer styles worldwide (you'll learn how in Chapter Two), British beer has been most influenced by a different kind of malt called caramel, or crystal, malt

First noted in brewing books around 1870, caramel malt gives beers an amber colour, but more importantly, a sweet, caramel flavour and a bit of body too.

Maybe you're thinking, haven't we already talked enough about amber-coloured malts? And yes, I certainly have said a good bit about them. But in this case, it's not just the colour that's key – it's the flavour.

Most malt is steeped, sprouted, then dried and kilned. But crystal malt skips a step.

Instead of drying, the grains are kilned when wet. The moisture, combined with the kiln's high heat, causes the sugars in the grain to caramelize, giving the malt a sweet caramelly crunch.

Crystal malt also adds body. As the caramelized sugars are a bit too complex to be fermented by yeast, they remain in the finished beer, making it taste sweeter and feel fuller.

This bit of weight became crucially important in British beers from 1880 onwards, when tax laws changed, making stronger beers much more expensive to produce. To save money brewers began producing weaker beers, but swapped in crystal or caramel malts to help add back in a bit of heft.

In the mid-1800s, IPA was Britain's most popular beer style, but by the end of the century it was on its way out. IPA was being replaced with less-strong and less-hopped versions known as "light pale ale" or "light bitter" and a new style of beer called "running ale".

Running ale was served fresh, only weeks after being brewed (a much quicker turnaround than the months or years of aging required for IPA) and eventually became the forerunner of modern-day cask beer. (We'll explore cask beer in the call-out box.)

While by no means traditional in the development of pale ales and British bitters (as they would have historically been brewed with pale malt alone), the inclusion of crystal malts became more widespread after World War I to the point that they are now considered a characteristic ingredient in these styles. Only a small quantity is needed though – too much and the beer starts getting a bit sickly sweet and raisiny.

>>

These days, British bitters encompass a broad range of colour, sweetness and strength, but it's generally agreed that ordinary bitter is a brewery's lowest-alcohol offering, best bitter is stronger with higher-quality ingredients, while strong bitters have the highest strength, but aren't necessarily the most premium (that's the best bitter).

A brilliant example of a best bitter, Harvey's Sussex Best, is brewed with pale ale malts, specifically the Maris Otter varietal, with a touch of crystal malt for balance. See if you can pick up on those sweet caramel notes that act as a counterpoint to the beer's bitterness.

While bottled versions are available, bitter really is best enjoyed on cask, so find a pub known for taking good care of traditional cask-conditioned beers and give this one a go for a sweet finish.

TASTE THIS	FLAVOUR	ABV
HARVEY'S SUSSEX BEST	CARAMEL, A TOUCH OF FRUIT, BITTER	4%

(STYLE)
BEST BITTER

ORIGIN
LEWES, ENGLAND

NOTES
ALTHOUGH BITTER IS IN THE NAME, THERE'S ALWAYS A PLEASANT AND BALANCING SWEETNESS FROM THE CARAMEL MALT, SO DON'T BE INTIMIDATED IF YOU THINK BITTER BEERS AREN'T FOR YOU. ADDITIONALLY THIS STYLE IS TRADITIONALLY SERVED ON CASK, AND – IN MY OPINION – BEST ENJOYED THAT WAY.

ALTERNATIVES
IF YOU'RE NOT NEAR A PUB, BOTTLED VERSIONS WILL DO. IF YOU CAN'T FIND HARVEY'S BEST, FULLER'S LONDON PRIDE OFTEN TRAVELS QUITE FAR FROM THE BREWERY SO THAT'S A GOOD SUBSTITUTE.

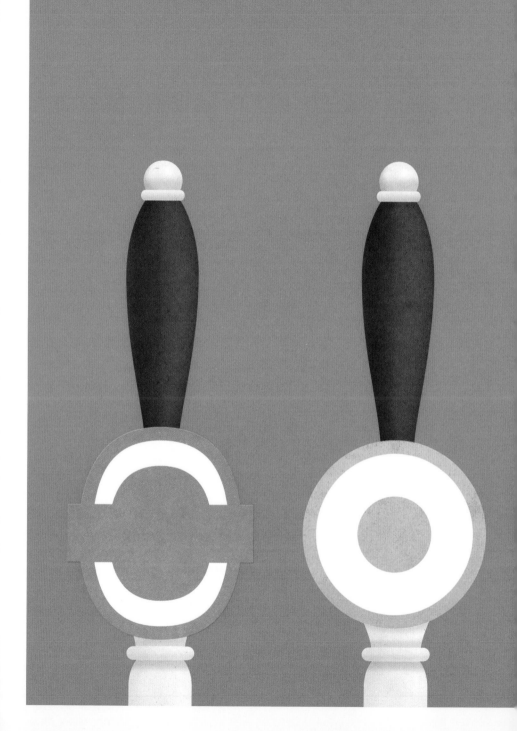

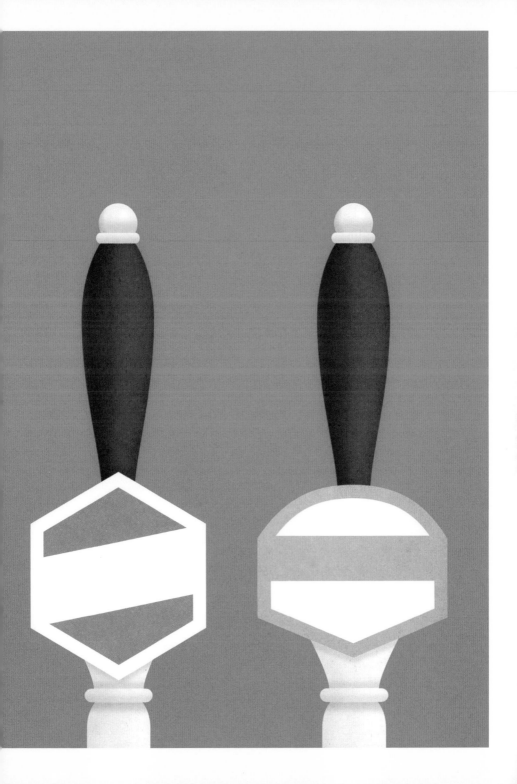

WHAT IS
CASK BEER?

I've mentioned British bitters are best enjoyed on cask, but what exactly does that mean?

Cask beer isn't necessarily a style of beer, but a method of dispense: cask-conditioned beers finish maturing in the vessel from which they're served.

When cask beer arrives at a pub, it's not yet ready to drink. Each cask contains live yeast and undergoes a secondary fermentation in the pub's cellar so it's important the cellar is kept at the appropriate temperature; 11–13°C (52–55°F) is recommended. This conditioning process allows the beer to mature and develop a mild, natural carbonation.

Cask beer, or real ale, is fresh, lightly carbonated, unfiltered and unpasteurized. It's a wonderful way to experience beer, but it takes care to cellar well. Cask beers also need to be consumed quickly once tapped for dispense (ideally within three days) otherwise off-flavours can develop.

Given these commercial challenges, it's probably no surprise that when a new method of dispense, kegged beer, was introduced in the 1960s it had a huge impact on cask-conditioned beer.

Kegged beers are conditioned and force-carbonated at the brewery

and arrive to the pub ready to serve. Additionally, they have a longer shelf life and require no special handling by pub owners.

For these reasons and more, cask beer began losing ground to kegged beers, so in the 1970s a consumer organization was formed to fight back. CAMRA, the Campaign for Real Ale, created a definition for real ale and sought to protect it.

While some may say their definition is a touch too traditional, it's possible that without their efforts, cask beer would be a thing of the past.

In addition to the aforementioned bitters, another style you may see on cask is mild ale, more specifically a dark mild. It's confusingly named, as historically any unaged beer was called "mild", but the modern-day mild is milder in *bitterness* than a British bitter. There are often regional variations in colour and strength, but the standard is copper to dark brown in colour and has been darkened and sweetened with brewer's caramel.

Interestingly, certain British beer styles were created with a specific dispense method in mind: some were draught (cask) products, like dark mild, while others were bottled products, like modern British brown ales. Again, there is a wide range of regional interpretations of the British brown ale style (southern versions were sweeter, while northern versions were drier and nuttier), but bottled brown ales are typically higher in strength and higher in carbonation than draught dark milds.

Although the terms "pale ale" and "bitter" were once synonymous, they've diverged over the years. Bitters are primarily thought of as draught products, while pale ales are the bottled versions. Did I mention that styles and their definitions can change over time?

These days, largely thanks to the craft beer movement (which we'll discuss in Chapter Four), all different kinds of beer styles can be enjoyed on cask in the UK. Cask beers will have a gentler carbonation and, as they're served slightly warmer than kegged beers, a fuller aroma and flavour.

So find a local pub known for taking good care of their cask beers, have an open mind and give one a go!

CHAPTER · 2 · TWO

1842–1980s
THE POWER OF PILSNER

You've had a brief introduction to pilsner malt and Pilsner Urquell, but there's a whole lot more to that story. Not only the beer's invention, but its impact.

The first truly golden lager, Pilsner Urquell, was produced in 1842 by brewer Josef Groll.

It's thought the burghers in Pilsen may have been seeking to trade on the popularity of England's pale ales at the time. Well, their plan worked. Pilsner was incredibly popular – and still is.

When most people think of beer, they think of a glass full of fizzy yellow liquid. You've got Pilsner Urquell to thank for that. Today, pale lagers account for the vast majority of beer consumed worldwide.

So how did one beer make such a big impression? It had a lot to do with timing.

Glassware became affordable in the mid-1800s, making beer colour matter in a way it hadn't before, as previously beer was consumed from metal tankards or ceramic steins.

Then by the late 1800s, new railroads let pilsner spread from city to city and country to country, while refrigeration enabled year-round brewing, and pasteurization helped the beer keep for longer, allowing it to travel even further.

By the turn of the century, the pale lager from Pilsen had taken the world by storm. And it didn't just spur on the development of more pale lagers. It impacted ales too.

From Germany, to America, Belgium and Britain, beers brewed around the world were going gold in order to compete. These are the styles shaped by the power of pilsner.

CZECH PILSNER
1842

Why was this pale lager from Pilsen so special? Nothing like it had been seen before.

It also helped that not only was Pilsen the perfect location because of the region's high-quality malt, hops and soft (mineral-free) water, the beer was produced at just the right time to take advantage of the Industrial Revolution's advancements.

Previously, beer colour didn't matter because it couldn't be seen. Most people would drink from metal tankards or ceramic steins, as glassware was largely unaffordable. That is, until the mid-1800s, when mass production of glass drinking vessels made beer colour oh-so-important.

Not only was Pilsner Urquell a beautiful golden hue, it was also crystal clear. The style's long lagering, or cold conditioning period, gives the yeast time to settle out, making the beer beautifully bright.

Imagine going from a ceramic stein of dark, murky beer to a glass full of bright, gold beer topped by a dense white head of foam. It's no wonder this new beer caught a few eyes.

The beer's appearance is only one aspect that helped lead to its domination, however. The other was its distribution.

Again, talk about timing: railway lines had just been built across Europe, allowing the sought-after suds to be easily shipped from Pilsen to neighbouring cities and countries.

Additionally, the first commercial refrigeration units were recently invented. Temperature control is key for breweries, from fermentation through to lagering. Without any ability to control temperature, many breweries could only brew during the coldest six months of the year. First installed at Munich's Spaten brewery in 1873, artificial refrigeration became the norm for most large-scale breweries by 1890.

Finally, glass bottles became increasingly more affordable in the 1880s, once mechanized production began. Previously, beer was transported and dispensed from wooden kegs or handmade glass or clay bottles, but all of these materials couldn't stand up to much carbonation. Machine-made glass bottles helped send bright sparkling beers around the world.

Beer could now be brewed year-round, distributed over large distances and, thanks to pasteurization, keep for much longer than previously possible. French scientist Louis Pasteur, after whom the process is named, realized beer's shelf life could be extended by briefly heating it, as this killed off any remaining microorganisms that could lead to spoilage. (This technology not only revolutionized the beer industry, but several others as well.)

These factors – railways, refrigeration, packaging and pasteurization – meant beer could now travel, extending one style's impact.

Brewers in Bavaria reacted first.

TASTE THIS PILSNER URQUELL (STYLE) CZECH PILSNER / CZECH PREMIUM PALE LAGER ORIGIN PILSEN, CZECH REPUBLIC	FLAVOUR CARAMEL SWEETNESS, SPICY HOPS, ASSERTIVE BITTERNESS	ABV 4.4%
	NOTES NOW MIGHT BE THE TIME TO NOTE THAT IN THE CZECH REPUBLIC, ONLY PILSNER URQUELL, THE ORIGINAL, IS CALLED A PILSNER. THE BROADER NAME FOR THE STYLE IN CZECH IS SVĚTLÝ LEŽÁK. BUT MOST STYLE GUIDELINES CALL IT A CZECH PREMIUM PALE LAGER OR CZECH PILSNER.	

ALTERNATIVES
IF YOU WANT TO TRY SOMETHING OTHER THAN PILSNER URQUELL, GIVE BUDWEISER BUDVAR A GO, ANOTHER LOCAL BOHEMIAN BREW (NOT TO BE CONFUSED WITH BUDWEISER FROM THE USA!)

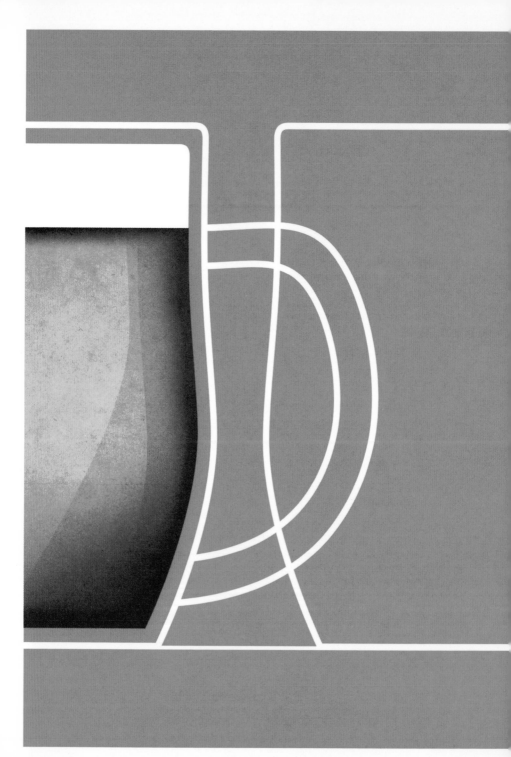

GERMAN PILS
1870s

Noticing what their neighbours were up to, Bavarian brewers tried their hand at producing a pilsner. But it didn't taste quite like the original.

The version produced in Germany had to suit the brewing conditions there, meaning different local hop varietals and more minerals in the brewing water. (The water in Germany isn't quite as soft as the water in Pilsen. Don't worry, we'll talk more about what this means in Chapter Three.)

To differentiate their version from the original Czech beer, the German interpretation is often called "pils", not pilsner. And truthfully, while it's said most modern pale lager is a riff on pilsner, we should really be saying pils – as it's actually the German version of the Czech pilsner that's most imitated.

Why? Czech pilsner is often brewed with a decoction mash to develop the deep gold colour and rich caramelization. But this is a rather time-consuming and labour-intensive process.

German pils is slightly lighter in colour, ranging from straw to light gold, as it skips that long boil. This means it's also lighter in body. Less malty rich, this style is balanced towards bitterness, which is further emphasized by the local hard water. (Mineral-rich water makes hops taste more aggressive.)

Overall, the German pils is dry and crisp with an elegant floral hop aroma and a lingering bitterness.

This style was first brewed in the 1870s, but no single brewery is clearly tied to the style like we'll see in other examples in this chapter. Plus, German pils didn't really take off at home until after World War II.

It took another few decades for German brewers to produce their own take on pale lager to rival Pilsen's.

TASTE THIS KÖNIG PILSNER	FLAVOUR CRISP, CLEAN, FLORAL HOP NOTES, BITTER	ABV 4.9%
(STYLE) GERMAN PILS		
ORIGIN DUISBURG, GERMANY	**NOTES** THIS STYLE IS KNOWN FOR BEING CRISP AND CLEAN WITH A FLORAL HOP CHARACTER (DISTINCT FROM THE SPICY NOTES FOUND IN THE CZECH VERSION). THERE'S A SLIGHT ASTRINGENCY FROM THE HOP BITTERNESS AND THE BEER HAS A LINGERING, DRY FINISH.	

PRE-PROHIBITION LAGER
1880s

Political unrest in Europe in the 1840s led many Germans and Czechs to immigrate to America, and they brought their brewing traditions with them.

As a former British colony, American brewing was largely influenced by English ales, particularly porter. But it soon became a land of lager.

Initially, immigrants brewed traditional dark lagers, like the Munich *dunkel* (which you'll hear more about in the next section). But things quickly turned pale, as the bright, bitter pilsner-style beers proved much more modern and fashionable than their heavy dark predecessors.

Starting small local breweries was important because they helped create a sense of community among immigrants. Not only were they able to enjoy a taste of home, but they could also preserve their culture and heritage.

But a few breweries had bigger plans. The idea of "national brands" became important as a way to create a shared identity among the different nationalities now calling America home.

German-born Adolphus Busch was one of several business owners at the time who dreamed of a brand that spanned the country. Busch partnered with his father-in-law, Eberhard Anheuser,

forming the Anheuser-Busch brewery in 1869. In 1876, Budweiser lager was introduced as the first beer to be shipped nationwide, thanks to our old friends refrigerated railcars, glass bottles and pasteurization.

This beer didn't taste quite the same as it would have back home, however. Brewing conditions in America differed drastically from those in both the Czech Republic and Germany. While immigrants brought their lager yeast and brewing techniques, they had to adapt their recipes to native malt and hops.

The type of barley that grows best in the USA is known as six-row barley. It's much higher in protein than European two-row barley and those high protein levels can produce a rather harsh flavour in beer. Six-row barley also includes plenty of enzymes, however, which made it possible to include local grains like corn and rice in the brew.

Corn and rice contain starch, but don't have their own enzymes to help make those starches accessible to the brewer. Combine them with six-row barley though and barley's enzymes will get to work converting all available starches to sugars, no matter their source.

Corn gives the beer a grainy, sweetcorn taste, while rice contributes a crisp, neutral flavour. Additionally, both help to thin out the body of the beer, so any harshness from the malt's high protein levels is rounded out. Traditional North American hops, like Cluster, would be used, adding a herbal, woody aroma to the grainy-sweet malt base. Making the American pre-Prohibition lager crisp, clean, and quite bitter.

As the name implies, however, the American lager emerged quite differently after Prohibition. (We'll explore the effects of this 13-year booze ban in the call-out box.)

Compared to most modern mass-market American pale lagers, the pre-Prohibition lager has much more flavour, more bitterness and often higher alcohol.

Prohibition, and a series of knock-on effects, led American lagers to become thinner, watered down and relatively flavourless – nothing like the punchy pilsner-style beers from which they once derived.

Homebrewers (folks who brew on a small scale at home) began to revive this

traditional American lager style in the 1990s.

Modern examples are likely to be all malt (like the lager I've recommended from California's Anchor Brewery), which is slightly different from the historical versions as they would have contained some rice or corn. But this is probably as close as we'll get to a taste of early American lager.

If you think you don't like pilsner because you've tried a modern American lager, give a pre-Prohibition style lager a go, then move on to a German pils or Czech pilsner.

You'll soon see it is much more than fizzy yellow liquid and will have a bit of insight into, and appreciation for, how this style took over the world.

TASTE THIS ANCHOR CALIFORNIA LAGER	FLAVOUR WOODY HOP NOTE, GRAINY, CLEAN, SMOOTH	ABV 4.9%
(STYLE) PRE-PROHIBITION LAGER	NOTES ALTHOUGH TRADITIONAL PRE-PROHIBITION LAGERS WOULD HAVE BEEN BREWED WITH SOME RICE OR CORN, THIS MODERN REVIVAL IS ALL MALT, BUT STILL USES TRADITIONAL CLUSTER HOPS, A NATIVE AMERICAN VARIETAL.	
ORIGIN SAN FRANCISCO, CALIFORNIA, USA		

WHAT HAPPENED
POST-PROHIBITION?

Prohibition was a 13-year-long ban on the manufacture, sale and distribution of alcoholic beverages in America, from 1920 to 1933. It forced many breweries to consolidate or close, leading to fierce competition and cost-cutting among the breweries that did survive, changing the flavour of American beer forever.

But there were factors at play before Prohibition. In the 1890s, the American brewing industry had already begun consolidating because of an economic depression. (There were more than 4,000 breweries in the USA in the 1870s; that number had fallen by half two decades later).

At the same time, the temperance movement – a social movement against the consumption of alcohol – was gaining momentum. And war with Germany meant German beers weren't looked upon very favourably (some going so far as to say drinking German-style lager was an act of betrayal).

Although the total number of breweries in the USA was in decline in the early 1900s, total beer output from these breweries was increasing rapidly through their newfound scale and efficiency.

When Prohibition put a stop to the production of alcohol, most small breweries were forced to close their doors. The larger breweries survived, however, by diversifying and producing goods like malt extract, soft drinks and "near beer" (beer that was less than 0.5% alcohol).

Due to the lost tax revenue and disastrous rise in organized crime, Prohibition was eventually repealed in 1933. But the Great Depression hit in 1929 and World War II was less than a decade away. Germans and their beer were under threat yet again and ingredients were rationed – proportional to brewery size. Again, smaller breweries took the hit.

Before World War I, the US had 1,392 breweries. After World War II, there were 476.

More than a decade without beer led most Americans to lose their taste for it, particularly beer's bitterness. After the wars, most remaining breweries were producing essentially the same beer – a crisp, clean and rather flavourless American lager. So how did they compete? Mass advertising, consolidation and cost-cutting.

By the end of the 1970s, there were fewer than 100 breweries left in America.

And a new beer style was about to take the country by storm – light beer.

Brewed with enzymes to make all of malt's starches fully fermentable, American light lager was even more dry, crisp and flavourless than the American lager from which it evolved.

Initially developed as a diet beer concept by Dr Joseph Owades in 1967, the idea didn't take off until it was relaunched a few years later as a lifestyle brand, a less-filling option loved by athletes. The first American light lager was Miller Lite and American consumers couldn't get enough.

Coors Light was launched in 1978, followed by Bud Light in 1981, which eventually became the number one beer brand in America.

Compared to the robust pilsner-style beers they once derived from, the post-Prohibition American lager and light lager are thin, highly carbonated and relatively flavourless with mass-market appeal.

They're both brewed with a large portion of rice or corn in place of barley malt, again to keep the beer as light and crisp as possible. (These ingredients add sugar, but no additional protein, so they won't bulk out the body of the beer.)

It's hard to believe the brewing industry could recover from this, but it did.

In the 1970s, what we know today as the craft beer movement led to a rediscovery and re-emergence of traditional styles from all over the world. But we'll save that story for Chapter Four.

MUNICH HELLES
1894

More than 50 years after the birth of Czech pilsner, Germany finally debuted their own golden coloured lager - the Munich *helles*, first produced by Spaten Brewery in 1894.

Helles simply means "light" in German, so it was the lightest coloured beer that a brewery would offer.

While the hard water in Munich makes the hoppiness of the German pils quite aggressive, the Munich *helles* was designed to keep this bitterness in check. How? It was brewed to be malt-forward instead (and has just enough bitterness for balance).

Best described as malty but not sweet, this thirst-quenching pale lager has a soft, rounded finish that practically begs you to order another glass.

Despite pilsner's popularity at the end of the 1800s, many German brewers were determined to stick to their staple, the Munich *dunkel*, or "dark", lager.

Dark brown in colour, the Munich dunkel has rich bready, toasty and sometimes chocolaty flavours from the darker Munich malt, but still remains easily drinkable. (We'll taste one in Chapter Five if you want to quickly peak ahead.)

Despite its years of history, it had nothing on the new kid on the block. If they wanted to stay in the game, German brewers had to go gold to compete.

But not all brewers gave in right away; some began brewing the new lighter-coloured beer next to its darker predecessor. This practice is thought to have ushered in the idea of brewing multiple beer styles at a single brewery, something we take for granted today.

Munich *dunkel* was finally eclipsed in the 1950s and today, Munich *helles* is the most popular beer style in southern Germany. A testament to the power of pilsner.

Next we see what happens when pilsner crosses the border into Belgium.

TASTE THIS	FLAVOUR	ABV
SPATEN MÜNCHNER HELL	GRAINY SWEET, JUST ENOUGH BITTERNESS FOR BALANCE	5.2%
(STYLE)		
MUNICH HELLES		
	NOTES	
ORIGIN	THE ORIGINAL *HELLES* OR LIGHT-COLOURED BEER FROM	
MUNICH, GERMANY	MUNICH, THIS BEER IS ALMOST TOO EASY DRINKING. BEST ENJOYED OUT OF A LITRE-SIZED DIMPLED MUG WITH A PRETZEL CLOSE AT HAND.	

BELGIAN PALE ALE
1905

I know the theme here is going for gold, but we've got one slight exception in this chapter, the Belgian pale ale, which isn't pale at all. It's amber. But the style was developed as a direct response to pilsner's popularity.

Pilsner-style lagers arrived in all-ale Belgium in the early 1900s and brewers there knew they needed to fight back.

In 1905, the Belgian brewers' guild launched a competition – the National Competition for the Perfection of Belgian Beers. Brewers were asked to create a truly Belgian original that was similar in strength to a pilsner (around 5% ABV), but significantly cheaper to produce and sell. It also had to be highly carbonated with a good head of foam.

73 breweries entered the contest and the winner was an easy-drinking amber ale called Belge de Faleau from Brasserie Binard. While the brewery has since closed, their beer became the inspiration for the new *Spéciale Belge* style, which proved to be a fast favourite among the Belgian working class.

Better known today as a Belgian pale ale, the style has a beautiful copper colour with a slight fruitiness and hint of spice on the nose, nutty, toasty flavours on the palate and a full, creamy body.

It's said today's best-known examples, namely De Koninck and Palm Speciale, were perfected after World War II with help from the Brits.

Belgian pale ale is actually surprisingly similar to a British strong bitter, but it has more Belgian yeast character and more carbonation. (Compared to other Belgian styles we're about to talk about though, the Belgian pale ale's fruity and spicy notes are much more subtle).

Although it's not truly pale, like most other beers in this chapter, it wouldn't have come about it if weren't for pilsner's influence.

TASTE THIS DE KONINCK ANTWERPEN PALE ALE	**FLAVOUR** FRUIT, A HINT OF SPICE, MALTY SWEET	**ABV** 5.2%
(STYLE) BELGIAN PALE ALE	**NOTES** SO POPULAR IN ITS HOMETOWN OF ANTWERP, DE KONINCK CAN SIMPLY BE ORDERED BY REFERRING TO THE GLASS IT COMES IN, CALLED A BOLLEKE. IT'S GOT A LOVELY SPICY HINT OF CINNAMON AND BEAUTIFULLY MALTY BODY.	
ORIGIN ANTWERP, BELGIUM		

BELGIAN TRIPEL
1934

Despite the success of the 1905 competition, Belgian brewers were up against a tough few years ahead. World War I led to the closure of many breweries, as copper kettles and other brewing equipment were requisitioned by the Germans.

But after the war, things began to look up for Belgian brewers. Strangely, thanks to the temperance movement. While Prohibition led to an outright ban on all alcohol in America, in 1919, Belgian cafes were prohibited from selling spirits, namely gin. So breweries started producing stronger beers to fill the gap.

Although monastic brewing traditions date back to the Middle Ages, the strong abbey and Trappist beers we're familiar with today are much more modern inventions. (And have a lot to do with that ban on gin!)

After persecution in France during the Napoleonic era, many monasteries relocated to nearby Belgium or the Netherlands. There they rebuilt their monasteries and began brewing again by the mid-1800s.

The Trappist abbey of Westmalle built their brewery in 1836 and, for many years, brewed solely for their own use, occasionally selling beer to the public from 1856 onwards.

The dark brown beer they brewed eventually became the beer we now know as Westmalle Dubbel in 1926, and it's considered a defining example of the Belgian *dubbel* style. Often brewed with a pilsner malt base and caramelized sugar syrups for colour and flavour, it's the yeast that really drives the characteristics of these Belgian beauties.

We'll delve into more detail on these particular yeast strains in Chapter Five, but for now, know that Belgian yeast often contributes notes of dark or dried fruit, spice and alcohol. Although the beer starts sweet, it finishes dry with hints of dark sugar, raisin and spice.

In 1921, the monks decided to sell their beer commercially, so a new brewery was opened at the abbey in 1933. The following year, a new super beer was introduced – the Belgian *tripel*. (It's said this beer was brewed with three times the ingredients than the monk's earlier beers.)

Deep gold in colour, the Belgian *tripel* is dominated by notes of spice, fruit, a hit of booze and a dry finish. Much like the *dubbel*, it's brewed with pilsner malt, but the monks also add pale sugar, which increases the beer's alcohol content without darkening its colour.

Tripels are strong, typically 7.5–9% ABV, but the clean malt character and firm bitterness (along with the high carbonation) helps hide the beer's strength well.

Westmalle Brewery is widely recognized for popularizing the strong golden *tripel* style and spawning hundreds of imitators worldwide.

It's likely no coincidence that Belgium's first pilsner-style beer was brewed in 1928.

TASTE THIS WESTMALLE TRIPEL	FLAVOUR SPICE, FRUIT, BOOZY, DRY FINISH	ABV 9.5%
(STYLE) BELGIAN TRIPEL		
ORIGIN WESTMALLE, BELGIUM	**NOTES** THE "MOTHER OF ALL *TRIPELS*", WESTMALLE IS CONSIDERED THE REFERENCE FOR THE STYLE. IT'S GOT EVERYTHING: SPICE, FRUIT, HOP BITTERNESS, A LIGHT ALCOHOL WARMTH, A CREAMY BODY AND A DRY FINISH. NO WONDER IT WAS SUCH AN INSPIRATION.	

MONASTIC BREWING TRADITIONS AND
TRAPPIST BEERS

Monastic life dates back to the 6th century when St Benedict founded the Benedictine order, which called for self-sufficiency. And since these early days, many monasteries have had breweries as a way for the monks to provide for themselves.

In the 12th century, however, St. Bernard broke away from the Benedictines and founded the strict Cistercian order, which called for manual labour. But this provision was largely ignored until the 17th century, when La Trappe abbey was founded in Normandy and the Order of the Cistercians of the Strict Observance was established.

Its monks were known as Trappists and their manual labour involved working in the fields harvesting wheat and barley and putting those grains to use in breweries within the monasteries.

In the late 1700s, during the French Revolution and Napoleonic Era, the Trappists were driven from France and resettled in Belgium and the Netherlands. They began brewing again by the mid-1800s and since then the reputation and availability of their beers has only grown.

There is a special distinction between authentic Trappist and abbey-style beers, however. Authentic Trappist products have a protected designation of origin, overseen by the International Trappist Association. To be advertised as an "Authentic Trappist Product" the beers must be made under the supervision of monks, within the walls of a monastery, with all profits going to the community.

Beers that do not meet these criteria, or that are brewed by secular commercial breweries under licence, are simply referred to as abbey beers.

The three most traditional Trappist styles are the *dubbel*, *tripel* and Belgian dark strong ale (sometimes called a *quadrupel*, or "*quad*" for short). Each brewery is said to have its own unique house character but there are similarities across styles.

All Trappist beers are bottle-conditioned, meaning a small amount of sugar and fresh yeast is added into the beer during bottling. This secondary fermentation creates the style's characteristic high carbonation and dry finish, as all remaining sugar is consumed by the yeast.

As discussed in the previous section, *dubbels* are deep brown in colour and have aromas and flavours of caramel and dark fruit, while *tripels* are a beautiful deep gold and are driven by spice. Finally, the Belgian dark strong ale exhibits the most house character. It's like a punched-up *dubbel* with more dark fruit, spice and booze. All of these styles are strong – on average 6% ABV for a *dubbel*, 8% ABV for a *tripel* and 10% ABV for a dark strong ale – but they hide it well.

While most Trappist styles fit into these three categories, there's one primary outlier – Orval. First brewed in 1931, the beer from Orval Abbey has its own distinct yeast character, but it's unlike that of the other Trappist strains.

Orval is pale in colour and fermented with a wild yeast strain, *Brettanomyces*, which gives the beer fruity notes when young, and earthy, funky, leathery notes with age. Much like other Trappist beers, it's dry and highly carbonated, but has a yeast character all its own.

Today there are now 14 Trappist breweries around the world: Achel, Chimay, Orval, La Trappe, Rochefort, Westmalle, Westvleteren, Zundert, Stift Engelszell, Mont des Cats, Spencer Trappist, Tre Fontane, Cardeña and Mount St Bernard.

BELGIAN GOLDEN STRONG ALE
1971

The ban on the sale of gin in cafes ushered in the era of strong, Belgian specialty beers we're familiar with today.

Another product of the times, Duvel, was first brewed in 1923 and was initially named Victory Ale to commemorate the end of World War I. The name isn't the only thing that has changed about this beer though. It changed colour too.

Inspired by the flood of British ales that came to Belgium during World War I, brothers Albert and Victor Moortgat set out to brew a strong dark ale, even trekking to Scotland to find the perfect yeast.

For nearly 50 years, Duvel was closer in colour to the English and Scottish ales that inspired it – a deep amber.

But with the popularity of pilsner-style beers, the Moortgat Brewery reinvented Duvel as a golden ale in 1971, creating a new beer style in the process, the Belgian golden strong ale.

While similar to the Belgian *tripel*, there are a few distinctions that help tell the styles apart.

Tripels are driven by spice, while Belgian golden strong ales are more fruit and hop forward with a drier finish. Additionally, golden strong ales are brewed to be lighter in colour and body than a *tripel*, but both have very high carbonation and hide their high strength well.

So what about the name? The saying goes a local shoemaker tried the beer, then discovered its strength, and declared it to be a real devil, or *duvel*, in Flemish.

Although Duvel may look like a pilsner, it certainly doesn't drink like one at 8.5% ABV.

For many years, Duvel was the best-selling specialty beer in Belgium. Note the word specialty. Even in Belgium, pilsner-style lagers still sell best.

TASTE THIS DUVEL (STYLE) BELGIAN GOLDEN STRONG ALE ORIGIN PUURS, BELGIUM	FLAVOUR FRUIT (PEAR DROPS), SPICE, CLEAN MALT, EFFERVESCENT WITH A DRY FINISH	ABV 8.5%
	NOTES A REAL DEVIL, THIS SPARKLING GOLDEN ALE HIDES ITS STRENGTH WELL. IMITATORS OFTEN INCLUDE A REFERENCE TO THE DEVIL IN THE BEER'S NAME AS A NOD TO THE ORIGINAL.	

THE STRONG BRITISH ALES THAT INSPIRED BELGIUM

Strong British beers, like the English barleywine and Scottish wee heavy, are said to have inspired the Belgian golden strong ale (before it went gold, of course).

The term "barley wine" has been used to describe the strong, October ales brewed on country estates since the early 1800s, but names like malt wine and malt liquor were used then too.

The first beer to be labelled as a barleywine wasn't seen until the turn of the 20th century: Bass No. 1 from Bass Brewery in Burton upon Trent.

Prior to picking up the IPA mantle from Bow Brewery in London, Burton brewers were producing a dark, strong, sweet, heavy ale then known as Burton Ale, which is the beer that modern-day barleywine derives from.

Today, barleywine is often the strongest beer that a brewery will produce and may even be vintage dated. The style is defined by its malt complexity; it's rich and chewy with aromas and flavours of fruitcake and a detectable alcohol warmth, which matures with a long aging. This strong beer is one to be sipped and savoured.

Although it was initially amber to dark brown in colour, even barleywine went gold. In 1951, Tennant brewery (now Whitbread) introduced a pale version called Gold Label. Paler versions tend to be more hop-forward and bitter, with complementary floral, earthy and marmalade notes from English hops.

Further north in Scotland, brewers there were producing strong ales throughout the 1700s and 1800s. They also brewed using the parti-gyle approach, discussed in Chapter One, in which multiple beers of varying strengths were produced from a single batch of malt.

The wee heavy, or "small strong", was the strongest of the Scotch ales, with export, heavy and light following in decreasing strength. (The name wee heavy comes from Fowler's brewery, who produced the defining example of the style.)

All Scottish beers are malt-driven with rich caramel flavours. They're not nearly as fruit-forward as similar English styles and are also lower in hops and a bit lower in alcohol.

A premium product, wee heavy was brewed for export, so it's no wonder this style travelled and had an influence elsewhere. Although it's not clear exactly which beer(s) influenced Duvel, we do know where the Moortgats sourced their yeast from – McEwan's brewery in Scotland.

I've recommended McEwan's Scotch Ale as the beer to taste here. I'm sure drinking it next to a modern-day Duvel it will be hard to find many similarities – besides the strength. But that just goes to show why learning the histories of our favourite beer styles can be so much fun... because their influences are often unexpected!

TASTE THIS FULLER'S GOLDEN PRIDE	FLAVOUR SWEET BISCUITY NOTES WITH FLORAL HOPS, WARMING	ABV 8.5%
(STYLE) ENGLISH BARLEYWINE	**NOTES** RICH MALT CHARACTER, WITH A BALANCE BETWEEN SWEETNESS AND HOP BITTERNESS. HOPS GIVE A NICE ORANGE NOTE TO COMPLEMENT THE FRUITCAKE FLAVOURS. WHILE DESCRIBED BY THE BREWERY AS A DARK TAWNY COLOUR, SO NOT TRULY GOLD, IT WAS AN INDICATOR THAT EVEN DARKER BEERS WERE LIGHTENING THEIR MALT BILLS.	
ORIGIN LONDON, ENGLAND		

ALTERNATIVES
THE ORIGINAL, GOLD LABEL, IS A BIT TOUGH TO FIND AFTER THE TENNANT BRAND WAS TAKEN OVER BY WHITBREAD.

TASTE THIS MCEWAN'S SCOTCH ALE	FLAVOUR TOFFEE, CARAMEL, WARMING	ABV 8%
(STYLE) WEE HEAVY	**NOTES** THIS STRONG, MALTY SCOTTISH ALE WAS THE SOURCE OF THE YEAST USED TO PRODUCE THE DEFINING EXAMPLE OF A BELGIAN GOLDEN STRONG ALE. YET ANOTHER EXAMPLE OF BEER STYLES' INTERNATIONAL INFLUENCE.	
ORIGIN EDINBURGH, SCOTLAND		

COLOGNE'S KÖLSCH KONVENTION
1986

The German city of Cologne has a brewing tradition that dates back to the Middle Ages. But as it's closer to Belgium than it is to Bavaria, Cologne's breweries produced ales, not lagers.

Those popular pale lagers increasingly encroached on Cologne though, so the brewers there had to produce something similar to compete. The beer we today think of as *kölsch* was likely developed in the late 1800s. It's light gold in colour and ever so delicate in flavour.

Why? Although it's brewed with ale yeast, which often give full-on fruity flavours to beers (we'll explore this more in Chapter Five), *kölsch* ferments at a cooler temperature than most ales, and then has a long cold conditioning, or lagering, phase that mellows out the flavours even more.

This unique style has subtle notes of fruit and honey and a grainy sweet malt base. It's clean, crisp, perfectly balanced and incredibly refreshing.

Because of its similar appearance to the pilsner-style lagers of the time, however, kölsch was under threat. In order to safeguard the style, local breweries lobbied the government for protection.

In 1986, the *Kölsch Konvention* was signed. Not only did it create a definition for the style, it also declared that only beer produced by the 20 or so breweries in Cologne and the surrounding neighbourhoods could be sold as *kölsch*.

It even detailed how the beer should be served, 200 millilitres at a time in a special glass called a stange.

That's only one part of this style's unique serving ritual. At tap houses in Cologne, there's no bar to order from. Take a seat and a waiter will stop by and drop off a glass of *kölsch* from a tray full of them.

An empty glass is replaced with a full one and a mark is made on a coaster to keep track of the quantity. Had enough? Just put the coaster over the top of your empty glass - the sign you're ready to go.

The power of pilsner pushed brewers to defend their traditions or develop new ones.

TASTE THIS FRÜH KÖLSCH	FLAVOUR SUBTLE HONEY, DELICATE, GRAINY SWEET	ABV 4.8%
(STYLE) KÖLSCH		
ORIGIN COLOGNE, GERMANY	**NOTES** WITH SUBTLE FLAVOURS, THIS STYLE IS BEST ENJOYED FRESH. I ENCOURAGE A VISIT TO COLOGNE. NOT BOTH ENJOY THE BEER AT ITS BEST AND TO EXPERIENCE ITS UNIQUE SERVING RITUAL.	

BRITISH GOLDEN ALE
1989

The power of pilsner eventually took over another all-ale country, Britain. But not necessarily in the way you might have imagined.

Pale lager washed ashore in the UK as far back as the mid-1800s. While some lager-only breweries were built in Britain, hoping to take advantage of the higher prices continental lager was sold for compared to English ale (in some cases more than twice the price), few had staying power and those that did faced an uphill battle at the pub.

First, British brewers were quick to react and re-tool their recipes. They began serving their "running" beers without a long aging period, which made them taste fresher and sweeter and helped them compete with the likes of lager.

The other challenge: lagers, which are fermented and conditioned cold, and meant to be served cold, were being served at cellar temperatures of cask ale (11–13°C or 52–55°F) and very few pubs had lager on draught. A warm bottle of lager is no way to win over your audience. It's no wonder it never took off.

So how did lager eventually win over England? It took a pretty cunning business plan and a Canadian lager named Carling. Carling's brewers

thought they had brewed a perfect beer for the Brits and assumed it would sell on quality alone.

What they didn't realize is most pubs in Britain were tied to breweries, meaning pubs could only sell a specific brewery's beer. So what did the business do? Acquire a load of British breweries, building their own empire of 2,000 pubs ready to sell kegs of Carling.

At the turn of the 20th century, sales of lager accounted for less than 1% of total UK beer sales. But by mid-century, it began to take off.

Brits began taking package holidays and became exposed to continental lager while abroad. Served colder and with more carbonation than traditional cask beers, kegged lager was refreshing and new. And drinkers began looking for it back home.

By 1971, lager, both kegged and bottled, made up nearly 10% of all beer volumes. By 1976, it was up to nearly 25% and by the end of the 1980s, lager made up the majority of UK beer sales.

So how did traditional cask brewers respond? A new take on British bitter was introduced that was a few shades brighter, the British golden ale.

Essentially a golden bitter, it's brewed with very pale or pilsner malt only; no caramel malts are used. Lighter in colour with none of the caramel sweetness found in the original, it's also well hopped, making it incredibly thirst quenching and refreshing.

First brewed on a small scale, Summer Lightning from Hop Back is often credited with getting the style off the ground in the late 1980s.

Initially brewed with English hops, most modern versions are now brewed with bright, citrusy American hops, which suit the style well. A summertime favourite, you may also see this style called a British summer ale or British blonde ale. And just to make sure it can still stand up to lager, it's often served slightly colder than traditional cask ales.

Despite the traditional brewers' best efforts, in the UK and around the world, pale, pilsner-style lagers still sell best.

TASTE THIS HOP BACK SUMMER LIGHTNING	FLAVOUR BITTER, GRAINY MALT, DRY FINISH	ABV 5.0%
(STYLE) BRITISH GOLDEN ALE	NOTES A REAL INNOVATOR, THIS AWARD-WINNING BEER AND BREWERY TOOK HOME BEST STRONG BEER IN BRITAIN AT THE 1992 GREAT BRITISH BEER FESTIVAL, JUST A FEW YEARS AFTER IT WAS INTRODUCED. BY 2005, A SEPARATE CATEGORY FOR GOLDEN ALES WAS INTRODUCED TO THE COMPETITION, SHOWING THE STYLE'S POPULARITY.	
ORIGIN SALISBURY, ENGLAND		

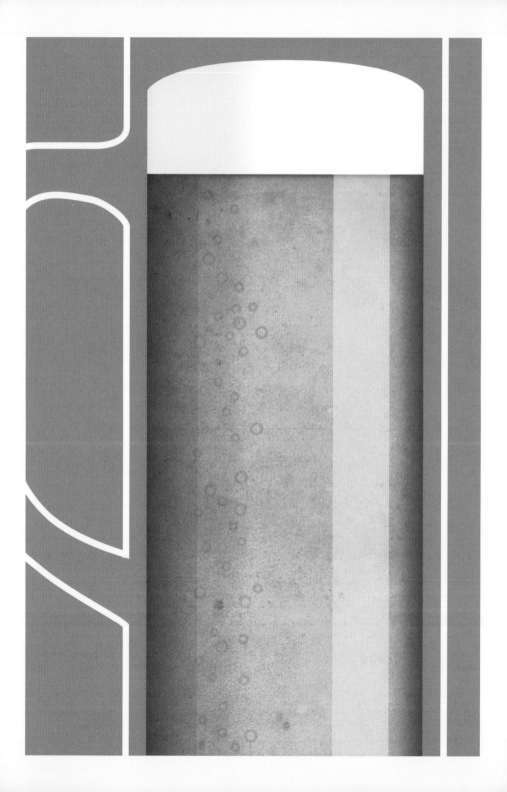

PILSNER TODAY

While the name "pilsner" (meaning of or from Pilsen) initially described Pilsner Urquell, the "original" Czech pilsner, today the term "pilsner" has a much looser interpretation, often used to describe any pale-coloured lager, regardless of its similarities to the original.

As we've already seen with porter, beer styles, or our interpretations of them, can change over time, even if the name stays the same. These days, just because it says "pilsner" or "pils" on the label doesn't necessarily mean the beer will have the complex, caramelly body of a Czech pilsner or the bracing bitterness of a German pils.

By knowing the true history of pilsner and its evolution we can start to appreciate its impact: spurring on the development of new styles, triggering the protection of others and eventually prompting a revival and rediscovery of traditional beer styles that may have otherwise been lost.

CHAPTER
3
THREE

1500s–1900s

LOCATION LOSES ITS IMPORTANCE

As you've just learned, technology, trade, changing taste preferences, war and more have all had their impact on beer's history. But one other key factor was location.

Brewers were only able to brew with the ingredients and techniques available to them.

While hops or malt could be shipped in, the limiting factor was always water. So it's no wonder certain styles developed in certain cities. Just think, if pilsner, the first pale lager, was attempted in London, not Pilsen, it might not have taken over the world the way it has today.

Water carries some weight when it comes to the historical development of beer styles, primarily because of the minerals it contains.

There are many different possible water profiles around the world, impacted by geology. But three key profiles have emerged as all-important in the history of beer.

In this chapter, we'll explore these water profiles, the cities they're found in and the styles they helped to foster.

As a note, as these are all classic styles that we've already come across in Chapters One and Two, instead of recommending the same beers again, I've included well-regarded examples of each style from somewhere other than its birthplace – to show you how our new knowledge of water chemistry enabled different beer styles to travel around the world in a way they never could before.

LONDON, DUBLIN AND MUNICH
1500s–1800s

The first water profile we'll take a look at can be found in London, Dublin and Munich, and was key to the styles that developed in these cities – porter, stout and Munich *dunkel*, respectively.

If you have a quick think, you'll notice all of these styles have something in common. They're all dark beers. Why did dark beers do so well in these three cities in particular? There was something in the water. Calcium carbonate, to be specific.

Dissolved into water as it travels over, under or through limestone bedrock, calcium carbonate makes the water supply slightly alkaline (heading towards the double digits on the pH scale).

This alkalinity doesn't interact particularly well with hops; it can make their bitterness overly aggressive and unpleasant. (If you recall from Chapter Two, German pils is more bitter than Czech pilsner because of the harder water. But don't worry, we'll learn what water profiles play well with hops next.)

So if hops aren't going to be the star of the show, make it malt. Even better, dark malt. When roasted, dark malt becomes slightly acidic, which helps to balance out the alkalinity of the hard, high-carbonate water.

Calcium carbonate gives water a temporary hardness, meaning it's removed by boiling. This helps it extract more colour from the malt, suiting dark beers even better. In London, Dublin and Munich dark styles flourished and their origin stories are inherently tied to their water supplies.

It's important to remember that none of this was understood at the time. We didn't fully understand water chemistry and how to adjust it until the late 1800s and we couldn't measure pH until the scale was developed by Søren Sørensen in 1909 (at Carlsberg Brewery, no less!)

Brewers (and consumers) just knew what worked and hence developed the styles we're familiar with today.

TASTE THIS DESCHUTES OBSIDIAN STOUT	FLAVOUR COFFEE, DARK CHOCOLATE, BITTER FINISH	ABV 6.4%
(STYLE) AMERICAN STOUT		
ORIGIN BEND, OREGON, USA	**NOTES** BREWED WITH ROASTED UNMALTED BARLEY, JUST LIKE AN IRISH STOUT, THIS AMERICAN STOUT SHOWS THAT BREWERS ARE NO LONGER LIMITED BY THEIR WATER PROFILES. ANY BEER STYLE CAN (SUCCESSFULLY!) BE BREWED IN ANY LOCATION.	

BURTON UPON TRENT
1830s

As you'll recall from Chapter One, London was the birthplace of the IPA, but it didn't become the global phenomenon we remember it as today until it was brewed in Burton upon Trent in the English Midlands.

Just over 130 miles apart, the brewers could surely access the same malt and hops, but the water they brewed with in Burton was completely different.

London water was hard with calcium carbonate, making high hopping rates taste rather astringent. Burton, too, had hard water, but it contained a different compound: calcium sulphate, also known as gypsum, which was sourced from the local wells.

Any sulphur-based compound can give off a bit of an eggy whiff and in Burton-brewed beers this odour became known as the "Burton snatch".

While the aroma was certainly distinct, the bigger impact was on the beer's overall flavour and appearance.

Unlike London water, the gypsum in Burton's water made the beer crisp and dry, helping to highlight the hops in a way that really allowed pale ales' bitterness to shine.

How? Gypsum helps to increase enzyme activity during mashing, enhances fermentation and improves the settling of yeast.

This means most of malt's starch is converted to sugar, which is, in turn, fully fermented by the yeast. With little fermentable sugar left in the finished beer, it's dry, has good shelf stability and is crystal clear. Additionally, calcium sulphate extracts less colour from malt than calcium carbonate does, producing an even paler beer from Burton's extra-pale malt.

This bright, sparkling, hoppy pale ale was really something. And, before the science was fully understood, there was plenty of speculation as to why.

In 1830, an organization called the Society for Diffusing Useful Knowledge claimed Burton brewers were adding dangerous chemicals to their beers to make them dry and bright. In response, the brewers hired chemists to analyse their brewing water, confirming it was calcium sulphate from the local wells all along. Coming out of the scandal unscathed, the region's pale ales became even more popular and Burton became recognized as the world's beer capital.

In the late 1880s, Bass brewery in Burton was the largest brewery in the world. (Top fact: Bass' red triangle logo was Britain's first ever registered trademark!)

>>

Burton's well water revolutionized the brewing industry in England and beyond. Not wanting to miss the boat, many London breweries moved to Burton to set up shop. Brewers elsewhere wanting a taste of the magic began to add gypsum to their brewing water. First practised in the 1860s, the term "Burtonization" was coined in 1882, and the process is still used by many IPA breweries today.

Yet again, brewing the right beer in the right place helped it make history.

TASTE THIS	FLAVOUR	ABV
GOOSE ISLAND IPA	CITRUS NOTES, GENTLE BITTERNESS, LINGERING MALT SWEETNESS	5.9%
(STYLE)		
ENGLISH IPA	**NOTES**	
ORIGIN	THIS ENGLISH IPA IS BREWED IN CHICAGO. CALCIUM SULPHATE (OR GYPSUM) IS ADDED DIRECTLY TO THE MASH TO "BURTONIZE" THE WATER. THIS HELPS THE HOPS, A COMBINATION OF AMERICAN AND BRITISH, PACK A PUNCH.	
CHICAGO, ILLINOIS, USA		

PILSEN
1842

Sometimes a great beer can be brewed in the absence of minerals altogether.

As I have mentioned already, the water in Pilsen, Czech Republic, is incredibly soft, meaning it contains hardly any dissolved minerals whatsoever. So why did this work?

It allowed the region's rich raw materials to truly shine. The high-quality local barley combined with a traditional mashing method, called decoction mashing, gives the beer a rich, caramelly malt body.

The local Saaz hops, which were used in high quantity, gave a distinct spice and bracing bitterness that wasn't pushed over the edge by any minerals in the brewing water.

The long lagering period allowed for the beer to brighten and gave plenty of time for carbonation to develop, leaving pilsner with a sparkling golden hue and billowy white head.

Had Josef Groll tried this recipe in his native Germany, it might not have been the success it was without the right water source.

The high levels of calcium carbonate in the water in Germany meant brewers needed to tone down their hopping rates, giving rise to the clean, balanced Munich *helles* style instead.

In Pilsen, everything fit, and it's no wonder this style had such an impact.

TASTE THIS FIRESTONE WALKER PIVO PILS	FLAVOUR FLORAL, SPICY, HOP-FORWARD, CLEAN	ABV 5.3%
(STYLE) CONTEMPORARY AMERICAN- STYLE PILSNER*	**NOTES** AN AMERICAN TAKE ON THE EUROPEAN ORIGINALS, CZECH PILSNER AND GERMAN PILS, THIS BEER IS BREWED WITH	
ORIGIN PASO ROBLES, CALIFORNIA, USA	GERMAN HOPS IN A BOLD, AMERICAN WAY. IT LOOKED TO PILSEN FOR THE INSPIRATION AND, IMPORTANTLY, ITS SOFT WATER PROFILE.	

*THIS STYLE IS FROM THE BREWERS ASSOCIATION STYLE GUIDELINES, NOT BJCP. A RELATIVELY NEW STYLE, IT INCLUDES AMERICAN LAGERS THAT HAVE A WIDER RANGE OF HOP CHARACTER THAN PRE-PROHIBITION LAGERS

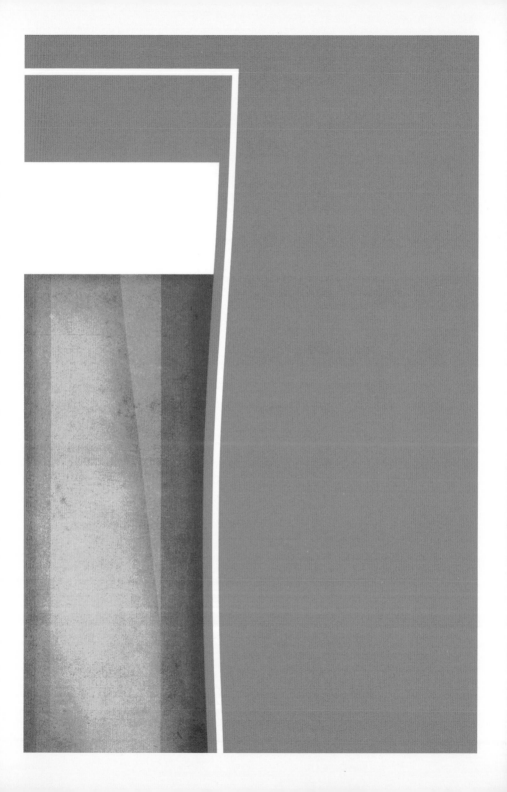

ANY WATER
ANYWHERE

By the turn of the 20th century, location had lost its importance.

When brewers learned how to Burtonize their water to punch up their pale ales, this was the start of modern brewing water treatment.

But they didn't only add minerals. Brewers also learned how to strip or remove minerals from their local water supply, enabling the production of pleasantly hoppy beers even in areas with high calcium carbonate.

It makes sense why, historically, brewers were known for one style – Bass for its pale ale, Guinness for stout and Pilsen for pilsner – that's all their local water profile allowed them to produce.

These days, most breweries produce a range of beers because they can alter the water chemistry as needed for the styles they plan to brew.

Additionally, breweries that were once tied to place, like Guinness, can set up satellite locations all over the world and can adjust the local water supply to mirror what's used in Dublin.

Now, we truly can brew any beer style anywhere.

CHAPTER 4 · FOUR ·

PRE-1000–2000s

HOPS MAKE HISTORY

Hops may be the hottest ingredient in beer today, but, believe it or not, there was a time when beer was brewed without them. Instead a mix of herbs called gruit was used to help flavour the beer, adding bitterness and balancing out the sweetness from the malt.

While the first written evidence of hop use in brewing dates to the year 822, it took another few hundred years before their use became widespread, likely because brewers had to discover how to best use hops in beer – hops require a long boil to impart their bitterness.

Once hops were adopted though, brewers didn't look back.

Not only were hops bittering, they also had a special preservative property. They prevented beer from spoiling, giving it a much longer shelf life.

By the 1500s, hops had largely replaced gruit as the main bittering ingredient in beer.

There were a few folks who held on to the old style of brewing; in the UK, unhopped "ale" was distinguished from hopped "beer" until the 1800s. But the Bavarians seemed to think hops were pretty important, declaring them one of only three ingredients allowed to be used in the production of beer in their

beer purity law of 1516. (Yeast wasn't understood just yet.)

Centuries after hops' first use in beer, we began to learn how to reproduce preferred varietals, then breed new varietals, giving a wide range of aromas and flavours to beer, in addition to bitterness.

Hops grow best in specific regions of the world, each producing different varietals with unique aromas and flavours. Historically, North American hops were only thought to be good for bittering, but all of that changed when a new hop was introduced in the 1970s that put America on the map for its aroma.

Perfectly timed with the beginnings of what we know today to be the craft beer movement, this launched hops into the limelight and made them the style-defining stars they've become.

YES, THERE WAS
A TIME BEFORE HOPS
Pre-1000

Hops are often described as the "spice" of beer, but before hops plenty of other bittering herbs – in a mixture called gruit – were used for seasoning.

The ingredients used to prepare gruit were kept a secret, but a few of the known ingredients were wild rosemary, yarrow and bog myrtle (also known as sweet gale), often mixed with other herbs and spices, from juniper and ginger to caraway and cumin.

Gruit was added to ancient recipes to provide bitterness, a bit of flavour and a mild preservative quality.

But it wasn't just an ingredient. It was actually an early form of taxation. (Hence why the recipe remained under wraps and it was thought to vary by region.)

The ruling class, be it the church or state, would hold what was called the "gruit right" (*gruitrecht*) and brewers were obliged to buy gruit as a way to pay their dues.

(It's said that in medieval Bruges, nearly half of the municipal revenue came from beer tax. So it was no surprise brewers were on the lookout for alternative bittering agents as a bit of a tax dodge! The laws caught up with them though with later taxes on hops.)

As you'll learn, once hops were heaped into beer, brewers discovered their superior preservative properties and gruit was gradually forgotten about.

That said, finding a beer brewed without hops today is a pretty tough task when you consider hops' popularity.

But a brewery in San Francisco, Woods Beer Company, has been brewing a hop-free ale, flavoured with hibiscus, bay leaf and yerba mate, since 2012. It may not be ancient, but it's likely as close as we'll get to a taste of history!

Next, learn how hops were adopted and why it all began in towns where beer was brewed for export.

TASTE THIS	FLAVOUR	ABV
WOODS BEER CO. MORPHO	TART, WINE-LIKE FRUIT AND BERRY NOTES	6%
(STYLE)		
GRUIT*		
	NOTES	
ORIGIN	DESCRIBED BY THE BREWERS AS A HERBAL ALE OR MODERN	
SAN FRANCISCO, CALIFORNIA,	GRUIT, THIS BEER IS BREWED WITH YERBA MATE, HIBISCUS	
USA	AND BAY LEAF. (NO HOPS.)	

*AS GRUIT IS A HISTORICAL BEER, IT IS NOT LISTED AS A STYLE IN ANY CURRENT GUIDELINES. BJCP'S SPICE, HERB, OR VEGETABLE BEER STYLE IS LIKELY THE CLOSEST FIT.

HOPS GET ADOPTED
1150

As hops grow wild and have several potential uses – from producing dyes to making medicine – it's impossible to say when they first made their way into beer.

Archaeological evidence suggests hops may have been used in brewing in Switzerland and France as early as the 6th to 9th centuries, but the earliest written record of hops being used to brew with dates back to the year 822 from an abbey brewery that was part of a Benedictine monastery in Corbie, northern France.

In a series of statutes on how the abbey should be run, the duties listed included the gathering of hops for beer production, implying hops were growing wild and that they were not yet being cultivated.

But it's unclear if the hops at this time were being used to preserve the beer or just to flavour it.

Evidence of the discovery of hops' preservative properties dates back to circa 1150 to 1160 from the writings of a Benedictine abbess in Rupertsberg, Germany, Hildegaard von Bingen. Her texts suggest that to produce beer with hops, a boil was required for hops' preservative properties to be revealed.

Why? Hops' preservative nature requires the bittering compounds within the hop's resinous core, the alpha acids, to go through a transformation brought on by boiling called isomerization. Alpha acids aren't very soluble, but these newly formed iso-alpha acids are, so they dissolve into the beer, bringing bitterness and preservative properties.

Even today, we're still unsure how these properties were first discovered, but their discovery was game changing.

As hops' importance to beer became clear, wild hops began to be cultivated. Again, it's not fully understood when or where cultivation began, but it's clear that cultivated hops were in use in the northern German cities of Bremen and Hamburg from the 13th century onwards.

Bremen and Hamburg were members of the Hanseatic League, a seaborne empire along the North Sea known for having a powerful navy and robust international trade.

The wealthy merchant class in these cities and other Hansa towns began brewing, then exporting, large quantities of hopped beer early in the 13th century. The beer needed to be stable enough to last the voyage. And what helped to prevent spoilage? A strong beer with heaps of hops.

>>

In Amsterdam, the new, hoppy imported beer proved particularly popular. Once Dutch brewers learned the tricks of the trade, they then began growing hops and exporting hopped beers to their neighbours in Belgium. Eventually, when Flemish immigrants arrived in England in the late 14th century, they brought their hopped beer with them.

Hansa towns not only became trading centres for hops, but for the best malt too. By the 14th and 15th centuries, the region's traditional brewing grain, oats, had largely been replaced by barley. But in Hamburg, the "Hanseatic League's brew house", wheat was used, as well.

For our closest estimate of this historical brew, I've recommended a strong, heavily hopped wheat beer from Germany – Schneider Weisse Tap 5.

This beer was first brewed in 2008 as a collaboration between Schneider Weisse in Munich and New York City's Brooklyn Brewery, bringing together a traditional German beer style, a pale *weizenbock,* and America's love of hops.

It may not be all that historically accurate, as hops were primarily used for preservation back then, not for their punchy aromas and flavours. But it's a nice little flash-forward to some of the hoppy American styles we'll come across shortly.

TASTE THIS	FLAVOUR	ABV
SCHNEIDER WEISSE TAP 5	FLORAL, FRUITY, BITTER, BOOZY	8.2%
(STYLE)		
WEIZENBOCK	**NOTES**	
	THIS STRONG GERMAN WHEAT BEER IS HIGHLY HOPPED, WHICH	
ORIGIN	ISN'T TYPICAL FOR GERMAN WHEAT BEERS, AS YOU'LL LEARN	
MUNICH, GERMANY	IN CHAPTER SIX. THE HOPS USED CONTRIBUTE BOLD FLORAL	
	AND FRUITY AROMAS, WHICH COMPLEMENT THE FRUITY	
	CHARACTER OF THE YEAST USED. BUT OF COURSE, IN THE	
	PAST, THE HOPS WERE PRIMARILY THERE FOR PRESERVATION.	

CULTIVATING NOBILITY
1538

While hops' preservative properties helped send beer abroad, brewers elsewhere couldn't help but notice some of hops' other key characteristics. From northern Germany, we head to the region of Bavaria in the south.

In 1447, the Munich city council issued an ordinance (thought to be a precursor to the well-known Bavarian beer purity law, the *Reinheitsgebot* of 1516) that limited brewers to using barley, water and hops only. (Yeast wasn't understood at the time.)

This ordinance made it pretty clear that by the end of the 15th century in Bavaria, gruit was a thing of the past.

By this time hops from both Bavaria and neighbouring Bohemia (present-day Czech Republic) were gaining a reputation for themselves. Why? It was becoming clear that different geographies produced different varieties of hops – some superior to others.

During the 14th century, the emperor of Bohemia made the exporting of hop cuttings from the region punishable by death. (It was understood then that this was a way to propagate more plants.) Similar restrictions were put in place in the German district of Spalt in the early 16th century and certified hop inspectors were then employed in hop markets in nearby Nuremberg.

In 1538, Spalt was granted the world's first ever hop seal, signifying the hops were guaranteed to come from their named region, as dishonest merchants were packaging up inferior hops and benefiting from the better hops' reputation.

A hop seal for the Bohemian varietal Saaz quickly followed, along with nearly 30 other hop-growing regions over the next 300 years.

By the 19th century, Bohemia was regarded as the world centre of hops, with Saaz setting the standard for all others. (Again, it's no wonder that Pilsner Urquell was such a success!)

A very select group of hops from Germany and the Czech Republic – Spalt, Tettnanger, Hallertau and Saaz – have now become known as "noble hops", because of their refined bitterness and the floral, perfumed or spicy notes they give to traditional German and Czech lager styles. (It's worth noting that despite their history and heritage, the term noble hops has a rather loose definition only coined in the 1980s.)

Modern-day genetic profiling of these hops has revealed that Saaz, Spalt and Tettnanger are so similar in makeup, it's likely they derived from the same plant. They express themselves differently, however, based on their growing

>>

environments. For example, Tettnang has the highest elevation and receives more rain and more sunshine than both Spalt and Saaz.

Saaz, highly prized for its aromatic qualities, is often described as spicy. While you've already tasted Saaz in Pilsner Urquell, a Czech pale lager, now it's time to see what it tastes like in a Czech dark lager.

While pilsner is so named because it's from the Czech town of Pilsen, similarly Budweiser Budvar is from Budweis, further south. While Budweiser Budvar also produces a pale lager, a dark lager would be more fitting historically in the 1500s, because – as you know by now – pale malts weren't around just yet.

This dark lager will have notes of roasted coffee and dark chocolate, with a spicy hop character from the local Saaz hops. (For comparison, why not try it next to their pale lager to see how the malt base changes the expression of the hops.)

It's worth noting that while early hop cultivation is poorly understood as it is, there's even less known about Bohemian hops, as a large fire in the town of Saaz in 1768 destroyed many historical records that might have given us a better idea. Today, few references to Bohemian hops exist before the 14th century.

Next, it's time to find out what happened when hopped beer washed ashore in England.

TASTE THIS	FLAVOUR	ABV
BUDWEISER BUDVAR B:DARK	ROASTED, BITTER, SPICY	4.7%

(STYLE)
CZECH DARK LAGER

ORIGIN
BUDWEIS, CZECH REPUBLIC

NOTES
THE TRADITIONAL LAGER STYLE BREWED IN BOHEMIA BEFORE PILSNER LED THE REGION TO GO GOLD, THIS DARK LAGER IS BREWED WITH 100% SAAZ HOPS. WHILE THE MALT WILL PROVIDE NOTES OF ROASTED COFFEE AND DARK CHOCOLATE, LOOK OUT FOR BITTERNESS AND A GENTLE AROMA OF SPICE FROM THE REGION'S RENOWNED SAAZ HOPS.

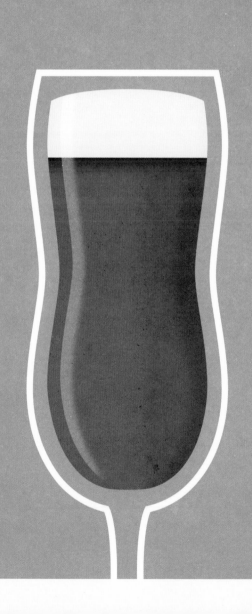

HOPS FLOURISH IN ENGLAND
1500s–1800s

While there is archaeological evidence that hops have had a presence in England for centuries, it's thought the first hopped beer wasn't brewed in England until the 1400s. Even still, those hops were imported.

Hopped "beer" was largely considered foreign, as English drinkers stuck to their traditional unhopped "ale" – a distinction that lived on in English drinking culture for another few centuries. (It's worth noting that just because ale was unhopped doesn't necessarily mean it was bittered with gruit; most English ales were brewed with three ingredients only – malt, water and yeast.)

By 1703, ale was said to be brewed with a small quantity of hops but was still distinguished from beer, which was highly hopped. (The distinction finally disappeared by the 1800s).

So how did hops eventually catch on? For several practical reasons. Prior to hops being introduced as a preservative, brewers would rely on alcohol to help keep their beers from spoiling. This meant high quantities of malt were needed, as malt provides the sugar that yeast ferments into alcohol (and carbon dioxide).

Beer brewers, those using hops, only needed to use about half as much malt

as ale brewers. And what they were saving on malt allowed them to justify the cost of hops and the fuel needed for their long boil.

English hop cultivation started in the early 1500s in Kent, southeast England, with hops brought over from Flanders. But these Flemish Red Bines didn't fare so well in English soil.

Instead, new varietals were introduced by taking cuttings of European plants or through natural cross-pollination. By the end of the 1700s, several varietals of English hops had come to be known – from Canterbury Whitebines and Farnham Whitebines to Goldings.

While Canterbury and Farnham Whitebines took after the German and Czech tradition of naming the hops after the regions from which they hail, Goldings have a different story.

Goldings are said to be named after one Mr Golding who spotted a superior hop plant (now thought to be a Canterbury Whitebine) growing nearby, cut it and propagated it – a process today known as clonal selection.

By the beginning of the 1800s, the hop was distributed across all parts of England, helping Goldings to become one of England's defining hop varietals.

The other defining English hop varietal, Fuggle, was thought to have grown from a seed dropped from a hop-picker's basket while eating lunch. It was said the hop was then named after Mr Fuggle, who, years later, cultivated the hop for sale. But the story appears too good to be true, as doubt was cast on it decades later.

While its origins are unclear, what is clear is Fuggle's impact on the British brewing industry. (Fuggle accounted for 78% of English hop acreage in 1949, before it was nearly wiped out by disease.)

So what makes these two varietals so special? They're most prized for their aroma and flavour, as both are relatively low in alpha acid content (around 3–4%). Goldings are celebrated for their floral, slightly spicy and honey-like aromas, while Fuggle contributes minty, grassy and earthy notes.

The aroma and flavour of these iconic British hops is forever linked to classic British beer styles like barleywine, pale ale and porter.

Fuller's 1845, a British strong ale, is hopped only with Goldings. The spicy and honey-like hop notes perfectly complement the fruity sweetness from the beer's amber malts. (A British strong ale is very similar in flavour to an English barleywine, but not quite as rich or strong.)

Despite their striking aroma and flavour, by the turn of the 20th century hops largely became valued for their preservative power over any other quality, leaving some British hops to fall out of favour.

TASTE THIS FULLER'S 1845	FLAVOUR FRUITY AND SWEET, WITH A DRY, SPICY FINISH	ABV 6.3%
(STYLE) BRITISH STRONG ALE	**NOTES** THIS BEER WAS BREWED IN 1995 TO CELEBRATE THE 150TH ANNIVERSARY OF THE FULLER, SMITH & TURNER BREWERY. IT'S BOTTLE-CONDITIONED FOR 100 DAYS, ALLOWING THE FLAVOURS TO MATURE. THE INITIAL AROMA IS REMINISCENT OF A FRUITCAKE, WITH A LOVELY DRY, SPICY FINISH FROM THE UNIQUELY BRITISH GOLDINGS HOPS.	
ORIGIN LONDON, ENGLAND		

HOP BREEDING BEGINS
1919

Up until this point, hops had been propagated by a process called clonal selection – the best growing hops were selected, cut and replanted to grow more of them. (Why? Hops don't breed true from the seed, meaning every seedling is genetically unique. Hence why cuttings were used instead.)

Hop growers would look for pest and disease resistance, high yield and, most importantly, a high alpha acid content. The sheer amount of bitterness, or keeping power, that hops could impart to beer was determined by their soft resin content, which was first measured in the late 1800s.

By the 1870s, American hops were being used by British brewers, but only for their high alpha acid content. Their aroma and flavour were actually disliked by most British brewers, so they'd be used early in the boil to impart bitterness and drive off any aromatic essential oils.

In 1906, Professor Salmon at Wye College in Kent set up the first hop breeding program, conducting crosses of different varietals to see what traits developed. His goal was to combine the high alpha acid content of American hops with the aromas of European hops.

Hop breeding requires patience. To proceed from the initial cross to commercial production, seedlings are assessed for resistance, grown in field tests, harvested and analyzed, used for pilot brews, then selected to grow on a commercial scale. All this can often take eight to ten years or more.

Professor Salmon made his initial cross of a wild North American female hop and male British hops in 1919. While the North American hop didn't take to its new environment, one of the seedlings did and was grown up for commercial cultivation.

In 1934, 15 years after the initial cross, Brewer's Gold was introduced to the world – the first verified cross or hybridization. Prized for its high alpha acid content, Brewer's Gold is the ancestor to all modern high-alpha hop varietals.

The recommended beer here, Crouch Vale Brewer's Gold, is "single hopped" with Brewer's Gold, meaning it's the only hop variety used in the beer. While Brewer's Gold was initially selected for its bitterness, it does contribute some nice fruity and spicy aromas to beer too.

Most modern varietals bred today trace back to those created by Professor Salmon just over 100 years ago. When Salmon began, hops contained 4% alpha acid on average. Today, alpha acid content can reach over 20%.

Large breweries often buy strictly on alpha acid content for practical reasons. The higher the alpha acid content in the hops, the fewer hops are needed in the brew. This also meant fewer hops needed to be grown.

Soon, characterful hops that didn't make the cut with their alpha acid content were left catering only to a very small audience.

While these new high-alpha cultivars took off in the United States and Canada, they never really caught on in England despite being developed there.

In Europe, the Czech Republic didn't start hop breeding until the 1960s and didn't release their first varietal until 1994. They feared the aroma of Saaz may suffer if hybridization was used to try to increase yield.

Hop growers in England and Europe stuck to their aroma varietals, but soon America got involved there too.

TASTE THIS CROUCH VALE BREWER'S GOLD	FLAVOUR FRUIT-FORWARD, BITTER, REFRESHING	ABV 4%
(STYLE) BRITISH GOLDEN ALE	NOTES THIS IS ONE OF THE FEW BEERS TO BE SINGLE-HOPPED WITH BREWER'S GOLD ALONE. AND IT'S A GOOD ONE, TOO! IN 2005 AND 2006, IT WAS RECOGNIZED AS THE SUPREME CHAMPION BEER OF BRITAIN AT THE GREAT BRITISH BEER FESTIVAL.	
ORIGIN CHELMSFORD, ENGLAND		

CASCADING INTO CRAFT BEER
1975

The United States got a late start in hop breeding because of Prohibition, but they did their best to catch up.

Prior to Prohibition, hop research had focused on plant diseases and yield, but afterwards the United States Department of Agriculture (USDA) began researching what it would take to produce foreign hops in the US. Then in the 1950s, they started their own hop breeding program. And we have it to thank for many of the flavours we're now familiar with in modern craft beer.

As mentioned, hop crosses take a long time to come into commercial use. One of the USDA's most famous crosses, known only as "56013" in 1955, was released to the public in 1972. Renamed Cascade, this hop came to define the soon-to-emerge craft beer movement in the States.

Cultivated hops had been grown in the US since the 1600s, again through the old process of clonal selection. By the 1970s, however, American hops were used primarily for bitterness, while imported European hops were used for aroma and flavour.

At this time, there were few breweries left in the States (Prohibition hit hard) and most remaining breweries had consolidated, producing watered-down, mass-market lagers that were nothing like the Czech and German pilsners that inspired them. Needless to say, hop bitterness, aroma and flavour weren't that big of a deal to most American brewers.

A young entrepreneur, Fritz Maytag, had recently taken over the failing Anchor Brewery in San Francisco, California, and was determined to brew a beer that was different. Inspired by a visit to England, Maytag set out to brew his take on an English pale ale. Anchor's Liberty Ale was first brewed in 1975.

With the help of a friend in the hop business, Maytag was connected with a hop grower in Yakima Valley, Washington, who was producing an experimental hop varietal (then 56013) for Coors Brewing Company. Coors was looking for American aroma varietals because of quality concerns with European hops. After brewing a batch with the new varietal, Coors' approval ushered in production of the first hop from the USDA's hop breeding program – Cascade.

Anchor also used the new Cascade hop in Liberty Ale, giving this would-be English pale ale a truly American character. Using a significantly higher quantity of hops than its English inspiration, it was more bitter than any beer on the market then. And it was bursting with citrus and grapefruit aromas.

Cascade truly put America on the map when it came to aroma and flavour hops and defined the palate of the early craft beer movement.

While Anchor's Liberty Ale may have been the first of the new American-style pale ales, they couldn't brew it often because they had a different flagship style they were best known for, Steam Beer (which we'll discuss in Chapter Five), which kept their production capacity limited.

Picking up the mantle, Sierra Nevada Brewery introduced their eponymous Pale Ale in the early 1980s. Also heavily hopped with Cascade, this beer came to define the American pale ale style.

So much for the English inspiration! The pale ale had been reimagined by American craft brewers and it was all about the hops. Bold, American hops at that.

TASTE THIS SIERRA NEVADA PALE ALE	FLAVOUR GRAPEFRUIT, PINE, RESIN	ABV 5.6%
(STYLE) AMERICAN PALE ALE	**NOTES** THIS BEER HELPED USHER IN THE AMERICAN CRAFT BEER MOVEMENT AND HAS INSPIRED COUNTLESS BREWERIES SINCE THEN. AN ENGLISH PALE ALE THAT'S HEAVILY HOPPED WITH WHOLE CONE CASCADE HOPS, IT'S A TRUE AMERICAN ORIGINAL.	
ORIGIN CHICO, CALIFORNIA, USA		

HOW DID THE CRAFT BEER MOVEMENT BEGIN?

The purchase of Anchor Brewery in San Francisco by Fritz Maytag in 1965 is said to have been a real tipping point in the craft beer movement's history. Maytag bought the old brewery to keep it from going out of business and to keep the unique beer style it was known for, Steam Beer, from disappearing. He wanted to show that beer didn't need to be bland to have mass-market appeal.

In parallel, in the 1960s and 1970s, young Americans travelled throughout Europe in a way they hadn't before – whether with the military or backpacking around. Inspired by the aromatic and flavourful beers they discovered (which couldn't be further from the lifeless lager that had come to define beer in America), many sought to bring these styles back home.

And some did just that once home brewing was legalized in 1979. Consolidation in the dairy industry made lots of disused equipment available, so homebrewers took it into their own hands to repurpose the kit for brewing.

New Albion Brewery in Sonoma, California is today acknowledged as America's first craft brewery. Founded in 1976 by Jack McAuliffe, unfortunately, the brewery only lasted six years before shutting its doors. But during that time, it inspired the next generation of craft brewers, including Ken Grossman, whose Sierra Nevada Pale Ale is regarded as the archetype of the American craft beer movement.

After an initial burst in the early 1980s, many other small breweries and brewpubs suffered the same fate as New Albion. Some were up against too grand a challenge, with little to no support from banks or investors, while others suffered from poor quality or inconsistency.

By the late 1980s, however, craft brewing took hold for good (albeit with a few more bumps in the road along the way). From a total of eight craft breweries in America in 1980, there were 537 in 1994 and nearly 7,500 in 2018.

The craft beer movement largely started with young innovative American brewers seeing what British beer styles they could turn on their heads. Why British beers? Many craft brewers started out as homebrewers and the only homebrew texts available at the time were from England.

But soon, brewers sought inspiration beyond British styles. And the craft beer movement grew beyond America, inspiring breweries to open across the UK, Europe and beyond.

Meanwhile in England, a consumer movement was taking hold. Traditional cask beers, which derived from the lower-strength running beers that proved popular after IPA's decline, were being replaced by kegged pale lager.

CAMRA, the Campaign for Real Ale, was formed in 1971 to help protect traditional cask beers. This spurred the development of the English craft beer movement, as small breweries began producing cask-conditioned real ales according to CAMRA guidelines. From there, British craft beer has only grown, with the UK reaching over 2,000 breweries in 2018.

Fittingly, the flavours of the early craft beer movement were largely defined by hops, hence squeezing in this explanation here. Ready to see what other styles were hopped up?

1000 1150 1538 1919 **1990** 1975 2000

REINVENTING THE IPA
1990s

The IPA originated in London in the 1780s, was perfected in Burton in the 1830s and reinvented in America in the 1990s.

At its heyday of Burton brewing, Bass Pale Ale truly defined the style. But after decades of popularity, the IPA was a shell of its former self: weaker, less bitter and essentially watered-down by the temperance movement, taxation and wars. By the 1950s, the English IPA was all but forgotten in favour of lower-strength bitters, as many brewers dropped the IPA style altogether.

Outside of England, IPA hung on a little longer. But the last remaining stronghold of the Burton IPA eventually disappeared in the late 1960s when US brewer Ballantine, the only IPA brewer to survive Prohibition, was sold.

As the craft beer movement was just kicking off, there were no current American or British versions of IPA to taste, meaning brewers could take the style in their own direction.

In the 1980s, brewer Bert Grant set up a brewpub – a facility that brews and serves its own beer on site – in Yakima, Washington. Conveniently, he was very close to America's hop fields and put their produce to good use. He's largely credited with reinventing the IPA for the modern craft beer movement when

he produced the first American beer to be labelled an IPA since Ballantine disappeared.

What began in a brewpub in Washington slowly spread along the West Coast, where the beer style was defined by a bold, bracing bitterness. Brewers became more comfortable challenging their consumers with hop-forward beers, and soon IPA became a permanent fixture in many breweries' line-ups.

Lagunitas Brewery became the first California craft brewer to make IPA its signature beer. Southern California breweries Pizza Port and Blind Pig were early IPA adopters too. But the style wasn't just limited to the West Coast. East Coast breweries got in on the game, too, led by Harpoon IPA and Brooklyn Brewery's East India Pale Ale. By the late 1990s, most craft breweries across the US were producing an IPA.

Many early IPAs were brewed with hops known as the 4 Cs – Cascade, Columbus, Chinook and Centennial – which all derived from United States Department of Agriculture's hop breeding programmes.

But as the competition to brew bolder, hoppier beers heated up, the first private plant breeding companies were developed and hop breeding became big business. To grow privately developed

>>

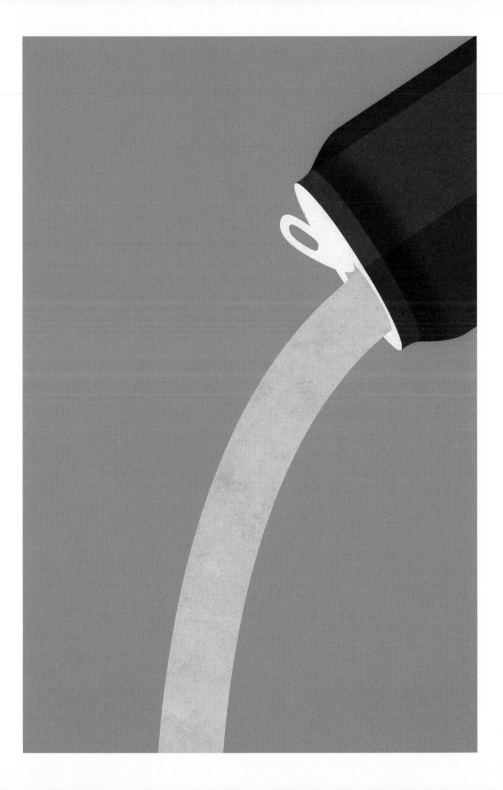

varietals, hop farmers need to acquire a licence.

Their rootstocks are not available in the public domain like the hops from the USDA.

Hop merchants began developing their own competing varietals, driven by brewers' desires for punchier aromas and flavours and big, bold bitterness. There are now hundreds of varietals that are becoming household names, like Citra®, Simcoe®, Mosaic® and Amarillo® – and more are being developed every year.

A technique called gas chromatography has enabled the identification of more than 400 unique aroma and flavour compounds to date. Often a combination of hops is used to achieve the right blend of bitterness, aroma and flavour.

Compared to the spicy, perfumy European noble hops or the floral and earthy English hops, American hops have aromas and flavours from citrus and tropical fruits, to resin and pine.

In order to allow the hops to stand out even more, the malt used in IPAs changed as the style matured. Initially evolving as an extra-hoppy pale ale, which was of course an American take on the English style, crystal or caramel malts were used. But they made the beer a bit too heavy and sweet, hiding the hops.

To improve the hop hit, brewers moved to pale ale malts only, which lightened the beer's body and let the hops shine.

Never ones to sit still, American craft brewers continued to reimagine the IPA by playing with how they used their hops and the quantities they used them in. Read on to learn how craft brewers continue to push IPA forward.

TASTE THIS STONE IPA	FLAVOUR CITRUS, PINE, RESIN, BITTER	ABV 6.9%
(STYLE) AMERICAN IPA		
ORIGIN ESCONDIDO, CALIFORNIA, USA	**NOTES** A CLASSIC WEST COAST IPA, THIS BEER IS ALL ABOUT BRACING BITTERNESS AND BOLD HOP CHARACTER. WHILE THIS WASN'T NECESSARILY THE FIRST MODERN IPA, I PICKED IT BECAUSE THE FORMER BREW MASTER AT STONE, MITCH STEELE, HAS LITERALLY WRITTEN THE BOOK ON IPA, SO HE KNOWS THIS STYLE (AND ALL ITS RICH HISTORY) INSIDE AND OUT.	

IMPERIALIZING IPA
2000s

Initially, IPA was highly hopped for keeping and the beer was aged for at least a year before it was sent abroad to help refine the hop flavour and soften the bitterness. (It was said unaged IPA was so bitter it was undrinkable. I wonder what drinkers in the 1800s would think of today's IPAs!)

While the hops would certainly have contributed aroma and flavour to the beer, as hop character tires quickly, the older the beer gets, the more muted the hop aroma and flavour becomes. That said, hops' essential oils certainly weren't prized by early IPA brewers the way they are today. Back then, it was all about the alpha acids and their preservative power.

These days, brewers are always looking for a way to push their IPAs to the next level. So what's an easy way to punch up the contribution of the hops? Add more!

And that's just what Vinnie Cilurzo did for his first beer at Blind Pig Brewery in Temecula, California.

In an attempt to mask any off-flavours from his less-than-perfect brewing kit, Cilurzo added more hops into his Blind Pig Inaugural Ale. Additionally, the beer was aged for nine months before serving. (That practice didn't last long though. Cilurzo's own IPA bottles today note to "drink fresh, do not age".)

First brewed in 1994, but not coined as such until the early 2000s, this double or Imperial IPA had twice the hops and a bit more malt than your standard IPA, upping the bitterness and the piney, grassy, and citrusy aromas and flavours.

This double IPA became the basis for Cilurzo's later brew, Pliny the Elder, at his own brewery Russian River. Since its introduction in 2001, this beer has become the reference for the style.

While breeding new, experimental varietals will always be a focus for hop merchants, they've also focused on creating new ways to deliver hop character to beer.

As mentioned in the Introduction, hops are added in during the boil to impart bitterness, but the boil drives off their aromatic essential oils. To boost their aroma and flavour contribution, it's best to add hops in towards the end of the boil, just after the boil, or wait until after fermentation to dry hop the beer.

Although all the rage today, dry hopping is nothing new. It has been used since the turn of the 19th century and early IPAs were definitely dry hopped. But newer products and techniques have dialled up its impact.

Historically, beers would have been bittered and dry-hopped with whole

>>

cone hops, which are dried after picking. As the dried hop cones can absorb a good bit of beer, however, this approach can lead to wastage, so many breweries have moved away from it. (Notably, Sierra Nevada is the largest brewer to still use whole cone hops only.)

Most other breweries use pelletized hops, meaning the hops have been dried, ground up, and compacted. Not only are they space saving and easier to store, there's also a lot less plant material and therefore less beer absorption and waste.

Developed in 1972, pellets have been around for decades, but they're a popular area for innovation. Producers of hop products are getting much more precise at concentrating the components of hops' resinous core, the alpha acids and essential oils. They've also developed pellets that dissolve and disperse more effectively, particularly in cold solutions like when dry-hopping.

This means less wastage and a more hop-forward beer.

One of the downsides of dry hopping is that the hop particles can contribute tannins, making the beer feel quite grassy and astringent on the palate. Another way to amp up beer's bitterness is to brew with hop extract, the concentrated hop resins only. As extract contains no other plant material, the beer won't become too astringent or tannic, even with heaps of hop bitterness and flavour.

Russian River's Pliny the Elder is brewed with hop extract, along with other hop products. Additionally, the body is thinned with sugar, which helps to increase the alcohol content without adding any sweetness or additional malt character to the beer.

Want to showcase hops? That's how you do it.

TASTE THIS PLINY THE ELDER	FLAVOUR FLORAL, CITRUS, PINE	ABV 8%
(STYLE) DOUBLE IPA		
ORIGIN SANTA ROSA, CALIFORNIA, USA	NOTES THE STYLE-DEFINING DOUBLE IPA, PLINY THE ELDER IS ALL ABOUT THE HOPS, THERE'S ENOUGH MALT PRESENCE FOR BALANCE, THOUGH. EXPECT FRESH PINE AND CITRUS NOTES AND A DRY, MOREISH FINISH.	

ALTERNATIVES
OFTEN WITHOUT A TRIP TO CALIFORNIA, PLINY CAN BE HARD TO COME BY (BUT IT'S CERTAINLY WORTH SEEKING OUT!) IF YOU CAN'T FIND IT, CHECK YOUR LOCAL CRAFT BREWERY FOR THEIR VERSION OF A DOUBLE IPA.

INNOVATING
WITH IPA

IPA innovation didn't stop with imperializing. Brewers have tweaked all aspects of the IPA recipe to see how the beer changes, developing new styles along the way. The one thing they all have in common though? Heaps of hops.

An early innovation was the black IPA, thought to have originated in the 1990s at Vermont Pub & Brewery by Greg Noonan. His original recipe was for a strong, roasty, winter IPA, which has been re-tooled and reimagined over the years by later brewers there. In the 2000s, brewers in the Pacific Northwest of the US began brewing dark, hoppy ales, but they called their version Cascadian dark ale.

These days, most black IPAs are brewed with a special type of malt called Carafa that has been dehusked prior to roasting. These dark malts increase the beer's colour and provide a mild roast character without becoming overly bitter or astringent. A black IPA should be dark in colour, but taste like an IPA, so any burned or harsh flavours are unwelcome. Piney, resiny hops fit this style well.

And yes, brewers have recognized the irony of the name black India pale ale. You may also see this style called an American strong black ale.

While some brewers changed their malt bill, others introduced alternative yeast strains. In 2006, Achouffe Brewery brewed a beer that is today thought of as the first Belgian IPA.

Best known for their strong Belgian blond ale, Achouffe used this beer as a base (upping the alcohol content slightly) and added in more hops. The hops used, Tomahawk, Saaz and Amarillo, bring citrus and grapefruit aromas to the beer and blend well with the fruity esters from the yeast. As Belgian yeast strains can be quite characterful (often producing high levels of fruity esters and spicy phenols), brewers need to be sure to select a strain that works well with the hops they have in mind.

The latest trend, hazy or juicy IPA, just became a recognized beer style by the US Brewers' Association at the 2018 Great American Beer Festival. That same year, BJCP developed a provisional style guideline, calling it New England IPA. The style is largely credited to John Kimmich's beer Heady Topper from The Alchemist Brewery in Vermont, which was first brewed back in 2003.

Dry hopping, adding hops after fermentation, has long been used to impart additional hop aroma and flavour. Regardless of whether whole cone hops or pellets were used, however, they'd leave behind a hop haze from leftover plant particles. This murky material would then need time to settle or be filtered out to produce a bright, clear beer.

Some brewers felt that by filtering their beers they were stripping away all-important hop aroma and flavour. So, for the love of hops (and the craft beer movement certainly does love their hops!), aesthetics were put aside in favour of aroma. Unfiltered, these hazy or juicy IPAs, as the name implies, have a hazy, almost murky appearance from the hop particles and yeast still in suspension. Some are also brewed with higher-protein grains like wheat or oats to ham up the haze even further and increase the beer's creamy mouthfeel.

Too much dry hopping can lead to grassy astringency, but when done well, hazy IPAs allow drinkers to experience hops' aromas and flavours (think bright, juicy tropical fruit notes) in a whole new way. Some even look more like a glass of fruit juice than a glass of beer!

From these examples, it's clear innovation and experimentation with IPA is likely to continue. That's how the craft beer movement began and is how it's bound to go on.

TASTE THIS 21ST AMENDMENT BACK IN BLACK	FLAVOUR ROASTED MALT, DARK CHOCOLATE, BITTER	ABV 6.8%
(STYLE) BLACK IPA **ORIGIN** SAN FRANCISCO, CALIFORNIA, USA	**NOTES** AN IPA BREWED WITH DARK MALTS, SOME BREWERS ADD THEM JUST FOR THE DARK COLOUR, WHILE OTHERS WANT TO GIVE THE BEER A BIT OF ROASTED CHARACTER TOO. THE STYLE SHOULD NEVER TASTE BURNED OR ASTRINGENT, BUT IT WILL CERTAINLY BE BITTER. (IT IS AN IPA AFTER ALL!) OFTEN A SEASONAL, NOT MANY BREWERIES MAKE THIS STYLE YEAR-ROUND, BUT FORTUNATELY FOR US, 21ST AMENDMENT DO.	

TASTE THIS HOUBLON CHOUFFE	**FLAVOUR** CITRUS, GRAPEFRUIT, BITTER, HINT OF SPICE	**ABV** 9%
(STYLE) BELGIAN IPA **ORIGIN** ACHOUFFE, BELGIUM	**NOTES** THE FIRST EVER BELGIAN IPA, THIS IS A STRONG BELGIAN BLONDE ALE HOPPED LIKE AN AMERICAN IPA. THIS BEER CAN BE PRODUCED IN REVERSE, HOWEVER, BY BREWING AN AMERICAN IPA AND FERMENTING WITH A BELGIAN YEAST STRAIN, GIVING THE BEER ITS FRUITY, SPICY NOTES.	

TASTE THIS THE ALCHEMIST HEADY TOPPER	**FLAVOUR** JUICY, CITRUS AND TROPICAL FRUIT, BITTER	**ABV** 8%
(STYLE) NEW ENGLAND IPA **ORIGIN** STOWE, VERMONT, USA	**NOTES** CREDITED WITH DEVELOPING THE HAZY IPA STYLE, THESE BEERS ARE OFTEN CALLED NEW ENGLAND IPAS AS A REFERENCE TO VERMONT, WHERE THE ALCHEMIST IS BASED. WITH ITS FRUITY AROMA AND HAZY APPEARANCE, THIS STYLE OFTEN LOOKS AND SMELLS MORE LIKE FRUIT JUICE THAN BEER.	

ALTERNATIVES
WHILE THIS PARTICULAR BEER CAN BE HARD TO FIND OUTSIDE OF VERMONT, THIS IS A VERY POPULAR BEER STYLE AT THE MOMENT, SO BE SURE TO CHECK YOUR LOCAL CRAFT BREWERY FOR THEIR TAKE ON IT.

CHAPTER 5 FIVE

3000 BCE–2000s
LAST BUT NOT LEAST, YEAST

The earliest evidence of grain-based fermented beverages dates back to nearly 9,000 years ago. And by 5,000 years ago the art of brewing was said to be well established by the ancient Sumerians. So it's hard to believe it was just over 130 years ago that we finally made sense of the microbe behind it all, yeast.

There were plenty of theories – starting with literal magic – but without a clear understanding of what was actually going on during the process we now call fermentation, it's no wonder this chapter is a bit of a bumpy ride.

Our journey starts in the ancient Middle East, then moves over to Europe, where much of this chapter is told. There, we bounce back and forth between Belgium and Germany, who, despite being neighbours, couldn't have more different fermentation traditions – from lager brewing, to the use of wild yeast and bacteria.

Despite brewing with ale yeast for many millennia, it was actually the discovery of lager yeast that led to the wealth of knowledge we now have about yeast and fermentation.

We'll explore the different species and strains of yeast that are used in brewing, including strains so unique they've come to define a particular beer style. Then we'll discover how craft brewers in America are reimagining traditional Belgian styles with our better understanding of wild yeast and bacteria.

Just a quick note about some changing terminology: historically, ale yeasts used to be referred to as top-fermenting strains, as they'd float to the top of the fermentation vessel and be collected from the foam on top of an actively fermenting batch. Lager yeast, on the other hand, settled to the bottom of the fermentation or conditioning vessel, so was referred to as bottom-fermenting.

These days, ale yeasts can be encouraged to settle, too, so these designations are less relevant. Instead yeast strains are best described by their fermentation temperatures: warm for ale and cold for lager.

YEAST'S ANCIENT ORIGINS
3000 BCE

In the ancient Middle East, the Sumerians were very fond of beer and the art of brewing was well established. They had an expansive range of brewing terminology and produced a range of beer styles. So it's pretty incredible to think it would take another 5,000 years for the agent behind all of this ancient fermentation to be revealed.

Yeast exists in several different environments; it's rather ubiquitous. But it's thought that the yeast present on fruit skins played an important role in ancient brews. That waxy haze on the outside of grapes is actually yeast. Hence why making wine must have happened quite naturally. As the fruit ages or is crushed, the yeast present on the skin will begin to process the sugars in the fruit and ferment them into alcohol.

While yeast can exist on barley kernels, as you learned early on about malt, its sugars are rather inaccessible. Evidence suggests that after malting the grains and preparing the mash, grapes or raisins might have been thrown into the brew to help get the process of fermentation going.

A 1950s archaeological dig, into what is believed to have been the tomb of King Midas, uncovered a 2,700-year-old drinking vessel that was thought to have contained a beverage brewed with barley, grapes and honey.

Inspired by these findings, in 1999 Dogfish Head Brewery in Delaware produced a beer-wine-mead hybrid and named it Midas Touch. While not a formal beer style, this modern take on an ancient ale reimagines one idea of how early beers were made.

Other historical evidence shows a special stick would be used to help kick start fermentation. Once the sugary liquid was prepared, the stick would be swirled through and, magically (a few hours later), foam would form on the surface, indicating fermentation had begun.

What we understand now is the stick harboured lots of dried yeast that would jump into action when introduced into the next brew.

Fermentation was thought to be a gift from the gods, one that could be ruined by evil spirits. Yeast, although not understood at the time, was referred to by the name "godisgoode".

The origins of the word "yeast" may relate to the Old English or German words for "froth" or "foam". Why? Once fermentation is active, a dense, rocky white head of foam forms on top of the beer, indicating the process is in progress. From the Middle Ages, brewers would skim the foam off the top of one batch and add it into the next, a process today called cropping and repitching.

Although they couldn't have understood it then, this process helped select only the most active yeast to carry forward into future fermentations. The characteristics of what would later become known as ale yeast, or more formally *Saccharomyces cerevisiae*, had been shaped over centuries.

But when new brewing techniques were introduced in Bavaria in the 16th century, a different species of yeast became the star of the show.

TASTE THIS DOGFISH HEAD MIDAS TOUCH	FLAVOUR HONEY SWEETNESS, BISCUITY MALT, DRY FINISH	ABV 9%
(STYLE) ANCIENT ALE*		
ORIGIN MILTON, DELAWARE, USA	**NOTES** DR PAT MCGOVERN, A BIOMOLECULAR ARCHAEOLOGIST, USED A SERIES OF CHEMICAL ANALYSES TO IDENTIFY THE MOLECULES THAT MADE UP THE ANCIENT RESIDUE INSIDE THIS 2,700-YEAR-OLD VESSEL. EVIDENCE INDICATED THE BEVERAGE CONTAINED BARLEY, GRAPES AND HONEY, GIVING US THIS UNIQUE BEER-WINE-MEAD HYBRID AND A POSSIBLE TASTE OF BEER'S EARLIEST HISTORY.	

*THIS IS NOT LISTED AS A STYLE IN ANY CURRENT STYLE GUIDELINES BUT IS A HANDY WAY OF DESCRIBING THIS MODERN TAKE ON AN EARLY BEER.

THE INTRODUCTION OF LAGER YEAST
1500s, Germany

We've heard a similar story before: beer quality was suffering so the people in charge decided to do something about it. But this was centuries prior to the invention of Pilsner.

In Bavaria in the 1500s, beer quality was taking a nosedive. Competition from the bakers for raw ingredients was pushing prices up. And brewing knowledge remained with the monks, who weren't too keen to share it with the Bavarian dukes. (The dukes recently stripped the monks of their brewing privileges so they could cash in on the tax revenue.)

All kinds of different ingredients were substituted in to help improve beer quality, but it was still suffering and that meant revenue did too. Inspired by earlier ordinances enacted in Munich in the late 1400s, the *Reinheitsgebot* of 1516, introduced by Dukes Wilhelm IV and Ludwig X, limited Bavarian brewing ingredients to barley, hops and water only. (The law said nothing about yeast as it wasn't understood yet.)

But even under the new law, beer quality issues weren't solved. Brewers did notice a difference in quality seasonally, however. Summer beer was subject to souring, while winter beer remained clear.

So in 1553, Duke Albrecht V, the son of and successor to Wilhelm IV, introduced

a new law banning brewing during the summer months altogether, from the feast of St. George to the feast of St. Michael (that's April 23rd to September 29th for the rest of us). This restriction on summer brewing was in place for the next three centuries.

To ensure they had stock available to serve during summer, Bavarian brewers began to store their beer in cold caves and cellars, kept cool with large blocks of ice from frozen lakes.

Over time, the beer would mature, stabilize, and brighten as the yeast settled out, and it would last much longer. Why? The cooler temperatures slowed down any spoilage. (Although not understood then, bacteria go dormant below a certain temperature range. Hence the principle of refrigeration.)

Meaning "to store", the German word *lagern* gave us the word "lager". (Light bulb moment!)

Cold storage not only gave us the name for this new family of beers, it also introduced us to a new species of yeast, one that that was able to ferment – not at room temperature – but at much colder temperatures, closer to freezing.

Its origins are unclear, but at some point in the past, *Saccharomyces cerevisae* (better known to us as ale yeast), hybridized with a cold-tolerant yeast called *Saccharomyces euyabanus*, giving rise to the species we know today as lager yeast, *Saccharomyces pastorianus*.

While ale yeast thrived at room temperature, much like bacteria it became sluggish at cold temperatures, which, conveniently, enabled the cold-adapted lager yeast to get to work. By reusing yeast from batch to batch, brewers selected for and shaped the characteristics of lager yeast over the years.

Today, all lagers are brewed with this cold-fermenting yeast and are said to have a "clean" fermentation character. As lager yeast ferments slowly at colder temperatures, it produces alcohol and carbon dioxide and that's it; no fruity esters or spicy phenols.

Cold-fermentation and cold-conditioning weren't the only approaches the Bavarians took to improve beer quality, however. Hops and high alcohol played a part, too,

as hops contain antibacterial compounds and high alcohol makes beer rather inhospitable to spoilage organisms.

Bavarian brewers combined all of the above to produce the beer styles we know today as *bock* and *doppel*, or "double" *bock*. Originating in the north German city of Einbeck, the bock style, originally brewed with ale yeast, became a lager when adopted by brewers in Munich in the 1600s. Brewed with dark malts that go through a decoction mash and a long boil, these beers are malty-rich, strong, and have a characteristic clean fermentation character.

Use of this new cold-adapted yeast strain caught on slowly, remaining localized to Bavaria and neighbouring Bohemia for the next few hundred years. (But you and I know that all changed with a golden lager known as Pilsner Urquell.)

While Bavarian brewers worked to prevent sour flavours in beer, next door in Belgium, brewers embraced them.

TASTE THIS PAULANER SALVATOR (STYLE) DOPPELBOCK ORIGIN MUNICH, GERMANY	FLAVOUR CARAMEL, CHOCOLATE, BREAD CRUST, ALCOHOL WARMTH NOTES *DOPPELBOCK* WAS FIRST BREWED IN THE 1630S BY THE MONKS OF THE ORDER OF ST. FRANCIS OF PAOLA IN MUNICH. (BETTER KNOWN TO US TODAY AS PAULANER BREWERY.) DEEMED 'LIQUID BREAD', THIS STRONG, MALTY-RICH BEER, NAMED SALVATOR, HELPED THE MONKS GET THROUGH THEIR FASTING FOR LENT. (YES, APPARENTLY BEER WAS ALLOWED.)	ABV 7.9%

SPONTANEOUS FERMENTATION
1500s, Belgium

This next style is as close to an ancient brew as we're ever going to get. Sure, I introduced you to a modern version of an ancient ale in the first section of this chapter, but that's because I wasn't sure if you'd stick with me any longer if you started with this style. Why? It's sour. And it's supposed to be.

Brewed since the 1500s in the Senne Valley, the region surrounding Brussels, Belgium, lambic is unlike any other beer. Often considered to be the world's oldest continuously produced beer style, its unique brewing process goes back to the way beer was fermented hundreds, even thousands, of years ago.

At the end of the brew, the hot liquid, known as wort, is funnelled into a wide, shallow vessel called a coolship. The large surface area helps to cool the wort quickly, readying it for fermentation, but for lambic it also serves another purpose.

In a process called spontaneous fermentation, the wort in the coolship is exposed to the night air, allowing the native microbes in the region, from brewer's yeast, to wild yeast and bacteria, to settle in and start fermenting.

The Senne Valley was once home to cherry orchards, and, as we learned earlier, where there was fruit, there was yeast. Although the trees are long gone, the microbes haven't moved. In fact, they've taken up residence in the nooks and crannies of the brew houses in the region. Cobwebs and dust are almost welcomed in these buildings, as they may be contributing to the house character of the spontaneously fermented beer.

After the wild yeast and bacteria settle in, the fermenting beer is moved into wooden barrels where it continues to age for months or years. More wild yeast and bacteria have taken up residence in these barrels, further contributing to the style's complexity. There's a beautiful dance between the various strains of yeast and bacteria present that give lambic its unique characteristics: sharp acidity, earthiness, light fruitiness and notes of hay and grass.

Saccharomyces, traditional brewer's yeast, will help the fermentation along. But it's the wild yeast *Brettanomyces* that gives lambic its "funky" flavours, which are best described as earthy or wet hay. It can often take six months for these flavours to develop, as *Brettanomyces* ferments very slowly.

In the meantime, different bacteria produce the style's sharp acidity. Both *Lactobacillus* and *Pediococcus* produce lactic acid (you may be familiar with it from the sharp tang of Greek yogurt). Although this may sound like a flavour you'd rather not find in a beer, it helps create one of the style's many layers of complexity.

Historically brewed with air-dried malt, these days the malt base is primarily pilsner malt, plus 30–40% unmalted wheat (which became a fixture of the recipe by royal decree in 1420). To ensure there is enough fermentable sugar for the wild yeast and bacteria, which continue fermenting for months or years, a unique style of mashing is used, a turbid mash. We won't go into details here, but the important takeaway is that it produces a wort that's high in dextrins – long-chain sugars that brewer's yeast can't ferment, but that are perfect fodder for wild yeast and bacteria.

Although the fermentation is said to be spontaneous, truthfully only specific strains of yeast and bacteria are welcomed, not all. So aged hops are also included in the beer; not for bitterness, but for their preservative properties. These days, temperature control is also key to help make sure only the right microorganisms are in action.

Despite its many differences to lager brewing, Belgian lambic brewers did have one thing in common with their counterparts in Bavaria at this time: lambic beers are only brewed in the winter and this seasonal restriction is still in place today.

Lambic is typically served after six months of aging. Poured flat, or uncarbonated, from pitchers at cafés in Brussels, this style doesn't travel well because it oxidizes quickly. So get yourself to Brussels to try some. Pale yellow to deep gold in colour, this wild Belgian wheat beer has a sharp, spritzy acidity and a dry finish.

Most lambic beer is often further aged, then blended with younger beer and bottled, creating a style called *gueuze*. (A typical *gueuze* blend is 60% one-year-old lambic, 30% two-year old and the final 10% has aged for three years.)

The young lambic contributes fermentables, while the old lambic contributes the funk. Overall, *gueuze* has more complex layers of flavour – think earthy, barnyard notes with a mellowed acidity. Additionally, it's much more highly carbonated than lambic, as fermentation continues in the bottle. (To keep all the wild fermentation processes in check, a rather sturdy glass bottle is needed, so this style didn't evolve until the late 1800s.)

Interestingly, not all *gueuze* producers brew their own lambic. *Guezesterkers*, translated as "cutters" or "blenders", buy in lambic from local breweries, age it in barrels on their own premises, then blend and bottle *gueuze* under their own brand name. This tradition was

>>

more common in the past, but modern blenders include De Cam, Hanssens and Tilquin.

Lambic can also be aged with fruits to create fruit lambic like *kriek* (which is aged on sour cherries) and *framboise* (which is aged on raspberries). Although it was likely produced on a small scale much earlier, fruit lambics weren't introduced as a commercial product until the 1930s.

As you can imagine, these artisanal products have come under significant threat by the factors that have taken many other traditional beer styles under. To protect these styles in today's market, a group of lambic and *gueuze* producers have created an organization called HORAL (the High Council for Artisanal Lambic Beers) with the twin goals of promoting and protecting their traditions.

While brewers in Brussels let nature decide what microbes made it into their beer, other brewers in Belgium sought particular strains to create their house character.

TASTE THIS BOON OUDE GUEUZE	FLAVOUR FRESH, BRIGHT ACIDITY, DRY, HIGHLY CARBONATED	ABV 7%
(STYLE) GUEUZE		
ORIGIN LEMBEEK, BELGIUM	**NOTES** AS LAMBIC DOESN'T TRAVEL WELL, IT'S BEST TO VISIT BRUSSELS AND GIVE IT A GO IN PERSON EITHER AT CANTILLON BREWERY OR NEARBY CAFE MOEDER LAMBIC. AGED AND BLENDED LAMBIC, OR GUEUZE, IS EASIER TO FIND OUTSIDE OF BELGIUM. CANTILLON IS A CLASSIC, BUT IS VERY HARD TO FIND IN THE USA AND OFTEN QUITE EXPENSIVE WHEN IT DOES MAKE IT THERE. BREWERY BOON'S OUDE GUEUZE IS EASIER TO FIND AND FRANK BOON KINDLY SHOWED ME AROUND HIS BREWERY IN LEMBEEK AND ANSWERED MANY OF MY BEER HISTORY QUESTIONS, SO THIS ONE'S A NOD TO HIM. THANKS, FRANK!	

SOUGHT AFTER STRAINS
1600s–1800s

Beyond Brussels, other Belgian brewers produced styles in which acidity was acceptable.

Flanders red and brown ales are each typified today by the beers of a particular Flemish producer: Rodenbach in Roeselare for Flanders red and Liefmans in Oudenaarde for old brown, or *oud bruin*.

This region had long been known for sour styles before either of these breweries was founded however.

In 1364, Emperor Charles IV of the Holy Roman Empire required the use of hops in brewing. At this time, the empire extended into Belgium, but only up to the Scheldt River. From this date forward, breweries to the east of the river brewed with hops, while breweries on the left side of the river, where Rodenbach and Liefmans were located, continued to use gruit or souring for preservation. (Today Liefmans is actually on the right-hand side of the river; it moved there in 1925. When it was first founded in 1679, it was on the left.)

Both Flanders red and brown ales harken back to the tradition of provision beers, strong beers that were brewed to be aged and developed a tartness over time.

Unlike lambic, which is brewed with a large portion of unmalted wheat, giving it a hazy yellow appearance, Flanders red and brown ales are brewed with Vienna, Munich, or other dark malts and are much more malt forward. Think nutty and toasty notes for reds and chocolate notes for browns.

Despite their similarities, the styles do differ – mainly in their method of aging.

Flanders red ale is fermented with a mixed culture of ale yeast and *Lactobacillus*, then aged in large wooden vats, called foeders, for up to two years. These foeders harbour the wild yeast and bacteria that help to develop the styles' complexity.

Many similar strains that are involved in lambic production are involved here, particularly *Brettanomyces* and *Lactobacillus*. But Flanders red is typified by the presence of acetic acid, or vinegar, produced by *Acetobacter*.

Acetobacter requires oxygen to be able to produce acetic acid, which is why the foeders are so important to this style. As the foeders stand upright, there is a small amount of headspace at the top that allows for oxygen exposure and, therefore, acetic acid production.

The acetic note blends in surprisingly well with the beer's darker malt character. But what jumps out of the glass is the style's fruitiness, think dark cherries and plums, giving this beer its nickname "the Burgundy of Belgium". Red wine lover? Try this.

Best exemplified by the Rodenbach brewery founded in 1820, most Flanders reds are blends of young and old beer. At Rodenbach, young beer is matured for five weeks, while old beer ages for two years in foeders. I've recommended the Grand Cru, but noted a few of their other blends below.

Even more malt forward is the Flanders brown style, also known as *oud bruin*, which is most closely associated with Liefmans Brewery.

Both yeast and *Lactobacillus* work together in a mixed fermentation, giving the beer a lactic tartness that mellows with its long aging period.

Oud bruin is not aged in oak, however. The beer has always aged in metal; initially copper, today stainless steel.

Again, the aged beer is blended with young beer before bottling to balance out the acidity and smooth any hard edges.

The darker malt character gives this beer notes of toffee, caramel and chocolate; there are also dark or dried fruit flavours that complement the sourness. It's an unusual mix of sweet and sour that proves quite pleasant to most drinkers. Look out for Liefmans Oud Bruin or Goudenband and see what you think.

It wasn't just the Belgians having all the fun. Many German producers – outside of Bavaria – brewed sour styles with a variety of different ingredients. (You'll learn more about these in Chapter Six.)

As lager brewing began to spread, however, breweries in Germany had to fight to keep their old traditions alive.

TASTE THIS RODENBACH GRAND CRU	FLAVOUR ACIDITY, GREEN APPLE TARTNESS, CARAMEL, VANILLA, OAK, MALT SWEETNESS	ABV 6%
(STYLE) FLANDERS RED ALE		
ORIGIN ROESELARE, BELGIUM	**NOTES** THIS BLEND IS TWO-THIRDS OLD BEER, ONE-THIRD YOUNG BEER. FOR A SLIGHTLY SWEETER STYLE, TRY THE CLASSIC, WHICH HAS MORE YOUNG BEER BLENDED IN. OR FOR THE TRUE HOUSE CHARACTER OF RODENBACH, GO FOR THE VINTAGE, WHICH IS UNBLENDED TWO-YEAR-OLD BEER DRAWN FROM ONE SINGLE FOEDER.	

HOW BRITISH BREWING
INFLUENCED BELGIAN
SOUR BEERS

When most people think of sour beers, they think of Belgium. And rightfully so. Today, Belgian brewers are keeping these traditional styles alive.

But did you know the Flanders red ale was actually influenced by British brewing techniques?

While not nearly as sour as today's sour styles, English breweries in the 1700s and 1800s aged porter for months or years and it developed an acidic "tang". Initially, the beer was long aged to allow the smoky flavours from the malt to mellow out. But as malting improved, the beer continued to age to acquire its prized tart, vinous, or wine-like quality.

By aging for up to two years in large wooden vats, beer would "stale" (thought to have derived from the word "stall" and the idea that the beer stood around a while). The beer would then be blended with "mild", or fresh, beer before serving to help round out the tartness and give the beer some carbonation or condition.

This is how most English porter was being produced up through the 19th century. In the 1830s, mild and stale beers would be blended at the pub to the customer's taste. Then by the 1860s, beers were pre-blended at the brewery before distribution.

So where did this acidic tang come from? Organisms like *Lactobacillus* and *Pediococcus* played a role in providing the acidity; but most of the beer's mature character is from the wild yeast *Brettanomyces* or "Brett".

Brett is believed to be endemic in wood, so the beer's long aging in wooden vats gave this slow-fermenting yeast strain plenty of time to produce its earthy, funky flavour.

Brettanomyces actually means "British fungus" and was named as such once it was discovered to be the cause of "spoilage" of British ales by researchers at the Carlsberg Laboratory in 1904. The Brits didn't consider this spoilage though. It was considered complexity, and it enabled British brewers to command higher prices for these long-aged, slightly sour styles.

While we don't think of porter as a sour style today, English porters had a big influence on one Belgian sour in particular – the Flanders red ale from Rodenbach.

In the 1870s, Eugene Rodenbach, the third generation to lead the brewery, went to the UK and learned about the aging and blending of young and old beers and decided to introduce those techniques back home in the production of Flanders red.

By the end of the century, stale porter
had fallen out of favour in England,
as preference tended towards lighter,
sweeter styles, so the practice largely
ended. But if you consumed a porter
during much of the 19th century, it
would have had a tartness to it.

Today, this tradition lives on in Flanders
red ales.

We'll talk more about our knowledge of
yeast, including Brett, and how it was
largely driven out of British brewing,
shortly. But I thought this was a good
time to point out Britain's sour beer
influence, despite no longer producing
any traditional sour beer styles.

KEEPING OLD TRADITIONS ALIVE
1800s

By the late 1800s, lager styles were spreading from Bavaria and Bohemia to the rest of Germany and beyond.Outside of Bavaria, Germany's southernmost state, most breweries still brewed the "old" style of beers with ale yeast. They had to defend their traditions or prepare for them to be washed out.

Düsseldorf's traditional brew is kept alive in *altbier*, in which *alt* means "old". (The name was first used to describe the style in the 1890s.)

We typically think of ale yeast as fermenting at warmer temperatures, so in this sense, *altbier* isn't *totally* traditional. Why? It's fermented at much cooler temperatures than typically used for ale yeast; it's also lagered, or cold-conditioned, at even colder temperatures.

Typically ale yeasts are very expressive, producing notes of fruit and spice from their esters and phenols, in addition to alcohol and carbon dioxide.

But at cooler temperatures, ale yeast cleans up its act. This copper coloured beer is cleaner and smoother than most ales, with minimal yeast character. It's also well hopped, making it a malty and boldly bitter ale, that's frankly unlike any other style in Germany.

The beer is brilliantly clear from its long lagering and has rich malt complexity to stand up to the bitterness and spice of the traditional German noble hops. Overall, it's smooth and sessionable at around 5% ABV.

If you'll recall from Chapter Two, neighbouring Cologne uses a similar approach with *kölsch*, which is cold-fermented with ale yeast and then lagered. But it's golden in colour with subtle fruit and honey notes and is nowhere near as bold and bitter as *altbier*.

Few versions of this style travel, so it's best to visit Düsseldorf's old town and enjoy this beer and its traditional serve – from small cylindrical glasses, much like *kölsch* – in person.

TASTE THIS	FLAVOUR	ABV
UERIGE ALTBIER	MALTY, BITTER FINISH, FULL BODIED	4.7%
(STYLE) ALTBIER		
ORIGIN DÜSSELDORF, GERMANY	**NOTES** ALTBIER CAN BE A BIT TOUGH TO FIND OUTSIDE OF ITS HOMELAND. SO YOU KNOW WHAT THAT MEANS – TIME FOR A TRIP TO DÜSSELDORF! ALTERNATIVELY, CHECK YOUR LOCAL CRAFT BREWERY TO SEE IF THEY'VE GIVEN THIS STYLE A GO.	

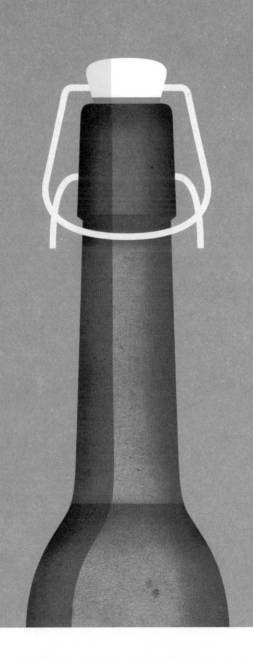

PUSHING THE BOUNDARIES
1840s

When lager landed in America with the arrival of German and Czech immigrants, brewers had to adapt their recipes to the available ingredients, hence how the American pre-Prohibition lager developed in the 1880s (as discussed in Chapter Two).

But a true American original was created just decades earlier because of the need to adapt, not only to local ingredients, but to available equipment as well.

During the Gold Rush of the late 1840s, explorers headed out west to northern California to strike it rich. And I'm sure their long journey led them to work up a thirst. Brewers attempted to brew a lager, but without cold caves, ice or yet-to-be-invented refrigeration, they needed to find another way to keep the fermentation temperature down for their lager yeast.

Enter the coolship. This time it wasn't used to capture the native yeast and bacteria (like with lambic), but for its original intention, as a large shallow surface to allow for quicker cooling of the boiled wort before fermentation.

San Francisco is known for its mild weather, which helped to cool the beer quickly, but still it reached nowhere close to the temperatures at which lager yeast prefers to ferment.

So brewers pushed the boundaries. They put their lager yeast to work at warmer temperatures, giving the beer a slightly more fruit-forward aroma than traditional lager styles. Why? At these higher temperatures, lager yeast produces esters, which give fruity aromas and flavours. (Normally ester production is reserved for ale yeasts, which typically ferment at warmer temperatures. Proper lager fermentation temperatures are too cool for ester production.)

They also used local ingredients such as six-row barley and rustic, traditional American hops. (Today Northern Brewer hops are most common.)

This unusual warm-fermented lager style became known as steam beer. Some say it's because of the steam rising from the coolships that would sit atop brewery rooftops across the city. Others say it's from the steam the wooden keg would let off when tapped, due to the beer's high carbonation. Whatever the real story is, it's a true American original.

Today, the style is best exemplified by Anchor Brewing Company's Steam Beer, which was reintroduced in the 1970s after the brewery was taken over by Fritz Maytag (who played a big role in the early craft beer movement, as discussed in Chapter Four). And it's a good thing, too, as they've got the trademark! All other breweries now need to refer to this style as a California Common.

Steam beer has a toasty, nutty malt character, an aggressive bitterness and woody, herbal hop character, with a light fruitiness on the nose. These days the style can also be brewed with a small amount of caramel malts, giving the style a nice caramel note.

If Maytag and Anchor Brewery hadn't saved steam beer in the 1970s it's possible it could have disappeared completely. Because what happened next was about to change brewing forever.

TASTE THIS	FLAVOUR	ABV
ANCHOR STEAM BEER	TOAST, CARAMEL, HOP-FORWARD, SUBTLE FRUIT	4.9%
(STYLE)		
CALIFORNIA COMMON	**NOTES**	
ORIGIN	A MODERN TAKE ON THIS MID-1800S STYLE, THIS BEER HAS GOT THE TRADEMARK AND SETS THE STYLE'S STANDARDS. (HENCE WHY ALL OTHER BREWERS NOW NEED TO REFER TO THE STYLE AS A CALIFORNIA COMMON.)	
SAN FRANCISCO, CALIFORNIA, USA		

MAKING SENSE OF MICROBES
1880s

At the end of the 17th century, Dutch microscope inventor Anton van Leeuwenhoek was the first person to observe yeast cells under a microscope. But back then it was thought that fermentation was a spontaneous process and yeast was the chemical by-product.

It wasn't until the 1830s that the living nature of yeast was revealed by three separate scientists.

Then in the 1860s and 1870s, famed microbiologist Louis Pasteur furthered our understanding of yeast in many ways.

First, he proved yeast wasn't a by-product of fermentation but the source of fermentation. Then in his 1876 publication *Études sur la Bière* (Studies on Beer), he discovered the cause of beer spoilage, and devised a method to prevent it.

By heating the beer to kill off the microorganisms it contained, the beer would be rendered shelf stable. Applicable far beyond beer, this process was named pasteurization in his honour.

Finally, by 1883, a pure single strain of lager yeast was isolated and cultured. This final step was the work of Danish scientist Emil Christian Hansen, who worked in the laboratory at Carlsberg Brewery. Initially, he named the strain *Saccharomyces carlsbergensis*, but it has

since been renamed *S.pastorianus* after Pasteur.

The ability to isolate, culture, and store yeast was revolutionary and forever changed the way we brew beer. Timed perfectly with pasteurization, refrigeration and the expansion of rail travel, lager yeast, and lager beer, could now be transported worldwide.

When Carlsberg's founder JC Jacobsen created the Carlsberg Foundation to oversee the management of the brewing science laboratory, he declared any discoveries made there would be for public use, not private gain. So these lager yeast strains spread quickly.

Compared to ales, lagers had a much cleaner and more consistent fermentation and a longer shelf life. Again, it's no wonder why so many classic ale styles were under threat.

Some brewers, particularly those in England, initially complained about the lack of complexity from single strain cultures. Previously, they'd been using whatever blend of ale strains they could re-pitch from the previous batch and it was soon discovered they weren't only brewing with *Saccharomyces*.

In 1904, Danish scientist Niels Claussen isolated the yeast strain responsible for the "spoilage" of British beers, naming it *Brettanomyces*, or "British fungus". Although considered spoilage by some, particularly lager brewers, British brewers believed Brett was essential for developing the correct flavour of long-aged beers.

Many British brewers held out, but by the mid-20th century, single strain cultures were adopted as the norm because of the improvement to beer's quality and consistency.

Incredibly, JC Jacobsen was good friends with Gabriel Sedlmayr of Munich's Spaten Brewery and it was Spaten's yeast strain that Carlsberg initially isolated and propagated. (If Spaten is sounding familiar, it's because Spaten's Sedlmayr gave us Munich malts, the modern day *Märzen*, and the Munich *helles* - so we've got lots to thank him for.)

Carlsberg recently re-brewed a modern day take on the first beer produced with this newly-isolated pure culture of lager yeast, a deep reddish brown lager called 1883, but unfortunately it was a short-lived experiment. It gives us a good indication of the style to try for a taste of history though.

Now's the perfect time to try that Munich *dunkel*. This Munich dark lager was what Spaten would have been brewing at the time when it donated a sample of its yeast (as it didn't introduce the Munich *helles* until 1894).

Unfortunately, Spaten doesn't export their *dunkel*, but neighbouring Munich brewery Hacker-Pschorr does. What are you looking for? Bready and toasty dark malts, hop bitterness for balance, and no noticeable yeast character at all. That's a clean fermenting lager strain for you. And what an impact it's had around the world.

While there isn't much diversity in lager strains, the same can't be said for ale yeast.

TASTE THIS	FLAVOUR	ABV
HACKER-PSCHORR MÜNCHNER DUNKEL	BREAD CRUST, CHOCOLATE, EASY DRINKING	5%

(STYLE)	NOTES
MUNICH DUNKEL	THE OLD STYLE OF LAGER BEFORE EVERYBODY WENT GOLD, THIS STYLE IS HARD TO FIND, BUT IT'S WELL WORTH SEEKING
ORIGIN	OUT. IT'S FULL OF TOASTY MALT SWEETNESS, WITH JUST
MUNICH, GERMANY	ENOUGH BITTERNESS FOR BALANCE. WHY NOT TRY IT NEXT TO A MUNICH HELLES TO TEASE OUT THE DIFFERENCES THE MALT MAKES?

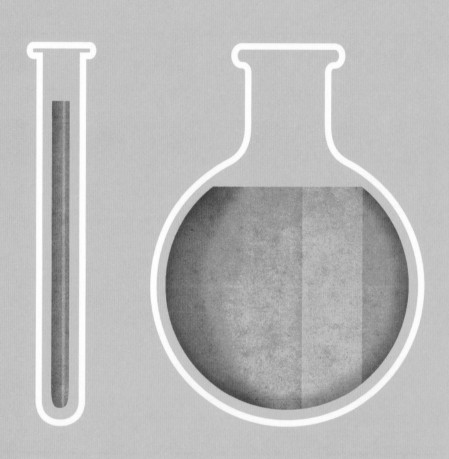

STYLE-DEFINING
STRAINS
1900s

With an understanding of yeast science and the ability to identify and propagate a single strain, centuries of unique flavours and characteristics could be teased apart and explained.

It may have been thought that the unique nature of many beers had something to do with the yeast used, but it took until the 20th century before we could actually isolate each strain and identify the compounds that were responsible.

When discussing style-defining yeast strains, a few beers come to mind: German *weissbier*, Belgian *saison* and Belgian Trappist styles.

German *weissbier* (which we'll discuss more in Chapter Six) differs from most beer styles because it's brewed with a large portion of malted wheat in place of malted barley, but it's not just the wheat that makes this style stand out.

It's brewed with a unique *weizen* ale yeast strain, which – in addition to the typical by-products of fermentation, alcohol and carbon dioxide – produces aromas of banana, bubble gum and clove as a result of its esters and phenols. Strange, right? (To get technical, an ester called *isoamyl acetate* gives the banana note, while phenol *4-vinyl guaiacol* is responsible for the clove character.)

But paired with the full, fluffy body and slight sweetness of a German wheat beer, these flavours fit in just right. What is also unique about this style is that it's traditionally served unfiltered, so the wheat and yeast haze remains in the finished beer. Hence the full and creamy body.

The Belgian *saison* is a farmhouse-style ale that was said to have been brewed to quench the thirst of fieldworkers during the active farming season. It is a very varied style; these days there are different colours and strengths. Some include a mix of grains (from barley and wheat, to spelt and rye), while others have added spices.

But what most examples of this style will have in common is the *saison* yeast character. *Saison* yeast is thought to be related to red wine yeast, giving it the ability to ferment at much higher temperatures than your typical ale yeast would be happy at (up to 32°C, or 90°F).

Additionally, it creates a characteristic aroma and flavour profile that is high in peppery phenols and rather low in fruity esters (if present, you'll find citrus notes like orange and lemon). As this strain can work at higher temperatures, it will continue fermenting, meaning the beer will finish quite dry (as all available sugars have been consumed) and very highly carbonated as well.

The style can appear quite similar to a Belgian *tripel*, but it often has a rustic, grainy quality and more spicy, peppery notes.

Saison has changed quite significantly over the years, but its modern archetype, Saison Dupont, took its current form in the 1920s. This style was at risk of dying out in the 1980s, as it was only popular with a rather local, and rather elderly, customer-base. In the 1980s, British beer writer Michael Jackson described the beer in his book *Great Beers of Belgium*, and a few years later, American importers got in touch. Since then the beer's popularity has only grown.

Finally, the Belgian Trappist-style beers, as discussed in Chapter Two, are also best defined by the yeast strain used.

The primary styles – *dubbel*, *tripel* and Belgian dark strong ale – are all typified by ale yeast strains that produce high levels of phenols, esters and higher alcohols (think rose or perfume).

Across the board, the phenols are spicy, peppery or clove-like. For the dark beers (*dubbel* and Belgian dark strong ale), esters often include notes of dark fruit, like plums, raisins and prunes, while in golden-coloured *tripels*, the esters are citrusy. When someone says a beer has a Belgian character, this is what they're talking about. (We briefly discussed this in Chapter Four with the Belgian IPA. Brewers need to be careful with the hop selection in that style, as some aromas and flavours can really clash!)

Thanks to our modern understanding of yeast, brought about in the late 19th century and expanded upon in the 20th century, many of these strains are now available as pure cultures. Brewers around the world can purchase these strains and recreate the traditional styles that have inspired them.

TASTE THIS SAISON DUPONT	FLAVOUR FRUIT, GRAINY MALT, SPICE, BITTER FINISH, DRY	ABV 6.5%
(STYLE) SAISON		
ORIGIN HAINAULT, BELGIUM	**NOTES** THERE CAN BE A LOT OF VARIATION IN THE SAISON STYLE, SO KEEP AN OPEN MIND. SOME HAVE ADDED SPICES, WHILE OTHERS ARE BREWED WITH BRETTANOMYCES (SEE THE CALL-OUT BOX LATER IN THIS CHAPTER). BUT ALL WILL HAVE A DISTINCT SAISON YEAST CHARACTER. HAVE FUN EXPLORING!	

3000 BCE | 1500 | 1600 | 1800 | 1840 | 1880 | 1900 | 2000

WILD GETS TAMED
2000s

If we're able to isolate individual yeast strains, well, why not bacteria too? Seeking to recreate the perfect blend that would have spontaneously settled into a coolship, many craft brewers are now introducing bacteria and wild yeasts to intentionally sour their beers.

You'd have thought with all we know about microbiology these days, you'd never have to see another sour beer again. But it turns out the layered complexity of these styles has some brewers attempting to reproduce them far from where they originated.

Brewers can now buy *Lactobacillus*, *Pediococcus*, *Acetobacter* and *Brettanomyces* and pitch them into their fermenter like a traditional ale or lager yeast strain, or introduce them into a wooden barrel for aging. These beers will then be aged and blended, like any traditional Belgian sour or wild ale, from *gueuze* to Flanders red.

Most breweries aren't letting microbes spontaneously settle into their fermenters, but that hasn't stopped a few from trying! Always up for experimentation, some American craft brewers are now trying to brew the ancient Belgian way.

Lambic and *gueuze* are both protected names; they fall under a European Union designation called Traditional Specialty Guaranteed.

While these laws don't apply in the USA, out of respect you won't see the words lambic or *gueuze* on any American-produced beers. Instead they're more broadly grouped into a catch-all category of American wild ales, which we'll delve into more in the call-out box.

As patience is required for most traditionally soured ales, there is a shortcut: you may see some brewers using "sour worting" to produce beers often referred to as "kettle sours".

In this method, *Lactobacillus* is added into the wort after the mash but before the boil. The bacteria will use up some of the available sugars, producing lactic acid in the process. Once the desired pH level is reached, the wort is boiled and the bacteria is killed off, so no further acidity is developed.

This is a quick, modern way to bring acidity to beer and is often used in modern versions of styles like *gose* or Berliner *weisse* (which we'll discuss next in Chapter Six). Quick and easy, it doesn't quite have the same complexity as aged and blended sour and wild ales.

It's incredible to think microbes considered spoilage organisms are still seen as sought-after strains in certain beer styles. As a result of the American craft beer revolution, these sour and wild styles are going through a renaissance

>>

and many breweries are trying their hands at them.

In 1999, New Belgium Brewing Company in Colorado became the first American brewery to produce a world-class sour beer. (It sure didn't hurt that their brew master, Peter Bouckaert, used to be the brew master at Rodenbach though!) La Folie, a sour brown ale, is also aged in oak foeders, like the beers brewed at Rodenbach, but this beer is slightly darker in colour and less driven by acetic acid.

Yes, sour and wild ales can be challenging at first, but take a bit of time and discover their complexity. (There are a few more recommendations in the call-out box for a helpful start.)

TASTE THIS NEW BELGIUM LA FOLIE	FLAVOUR SHARP, SOUR, GREEN APPLE, LIGHT CARAMEL SWEETNESS	ABV 7.0%

(STYLE)
AMERICAN WILD ALE:
WILD SPECIALTY BEER

NOTES

ORIGIN
FORT COLLINS, COLORADO, USA

THIS SOUR BROWN ALE HAS BEEN AGED IN FOEDERS, LARGE WOODEN VATS THAT ARE TRADITIONALLY USED TO AGE THE FLANDERS RED BEER STYLE. CONVENIENTLY, THE BREW MASTER AT NEW BELGIUM USED TO WORK AT RODENBACH, THE BREWERY BEST KNOWN FOR THE FLANDERS RED STYLE, BUT HE'S PUT HIS OWN SPIN ON LA FOLIE, USING DARKER MALTS FOR A SLIGHTLY MORE MALT-FORWARD FLAVOUR WITH LOTS OF BRIGHT, GREEN APPLE ACIDITY.

AMERICAN
WILD ALES

In the 1990s, there were just a handful of American craft breweries experimenting with wild and sour ales. In 2002, the Great American Beer Festival introduced its first sour beer category (Belgian-style sour ale), a good indicator that a style was gaining momentum. From that first year with 13 entries, interest in these types of beers has only grown.

American wild ales are broadly grouped into three styles according to the BJCP guidelines: beers brewed with Brettanomyces, beers brewed using a mixed culture fermentation and mixed culture beers that contain additional ingredients like fruit or spices, known as wild specialty beers.

Wild doesn't necessarily imply these beers have been spontaneously fermented – as most haven't. Instead it means non-traditional yeast has been used.

Brett beers include examples that have been brewed with traditional brewer's yeast and finished with Brett, or those fermented with Brettanomyces alone. These beers tend to be drier and lighter in body, as Brettanomyces can use up sugars that Saccharomyces can't.

Brett contributes tropical fruit notes when young. Then with time, a funkier character develops, giving those earthy, leathery notes. Much like traditional brewer's yeast, there are different strains of Brettanomyces that help contribute a range of aromas and flavours.

Mixed fermentation sour beers are the American craft brewers' interpretation of traditional Belgian styles. They're often brewed with some combination of Brettanomyces, Lactobacillus, Pediococcus and Acetobacter, then aged and blended.

Finally, the specialty versions are similar to the above, but have fruit, spices or other ingredients added. A great example is Russian River's Supplication, a mixed fermentation beer aged in Pinot Noir barrels with cherries. Talk about complex.

While the styles in Belgium are centuries old and well defined, American craft brewers are finding what fits for them, with each developing their own unique approach.

New Belgium matures many of their beers in foeders, no doubt influenced by their brew master's time at Rodenbach.

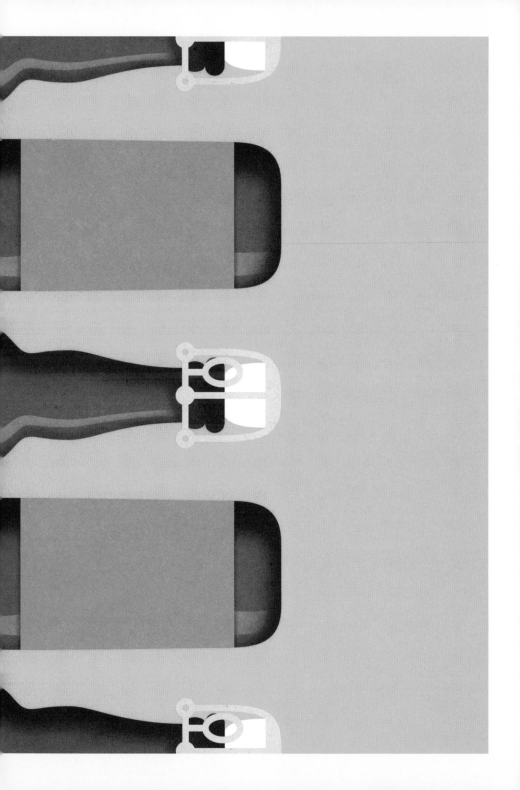

Russian River's sour and wild ales
are often aged in wine barrels, as
the brewery is located near northern
California's premier wine regions and
the owner and brew master, Vinnie
Cilurzo, had a wine-making background
before the transition to beer.

The Bruery experiments with barrel
aging, not only to produce sour and
wild beers, but also to produce strong,
spirituous beers that have been aged
in barrels that previously held bourbon
(we'll talk more about this in the
Conclusion). Their Tart of Darkness is a
sour stout aged in second-use bourbon
barrels with their house culture of yeast
and bacteria.

Again, as we discussed about beer
styles at the very beginning of the
book, they're mostly used so brewers
can give consumers an idea of what to
expect from the beer in front of them.

With sour and wild beers, there are
rough guidelines, but breweries across
the country, and the world, are having
fun experimenting in all kinds of ways.
So allow these styles a bit of breathing
room, but be sure to give them a go.

TASTE THIS BOULEVARD SAISON BRETT	FLAVOUR CITRUS, EARTHY, FUNKY	ABV 8.5%
(STYLE) BRETT BEER **ORIGIN** KANSAS CITY, MISSOURI, USA	**NOTES** BOULEVARD BREWING CO PRODUCES A SAISON THEY'RE WELL KNOWN FOR, TANK 7. TO PRODUCE SAISON BRETT, THEY REFERMENT TANK 7 WITH BRETTANOMYCES AND DRY HOP IT WITH CITRUSY HOPS LIKE AMARILLO TO PLAY UP BRETT'S TROPICAL FRUIT NOTES. IT'S DRIER AND MORE HIGHLY CARBONATED THAN THE ORIGINAL. TRY THEM SIDE-BY-SIDE TO REALLY GET AN IDEA OF HOW BRETT IMPACTS A BEER.	

TASTE THIS THE BRUERY TART OF DARKNESS	FLAVOUR TART, PLUMS, ROASTY, VANILLA	ABV 6.6%
(STYLE) MIXED FERMENTATION SOUR BEER **ORIGIN** PLACENTIA, CALIFORNIA, USA	**NOTES** A SOUR STOUT, THIS DARK BEER IS AGED IN SECOND-USE BOURBON BARRELS INOCULATED WITH MICROBES LIKE LACTOBACILLUS, PEDIOCOCCUS AND BRETTANOMYCES. IT'S GOT RICH ROASTY, COFFEE NOTES THAT PLAY WELL WITH THE BEER'S SOUR CHARACTER. AS THE BARRELS HAVE PREVIOUSLY HELD BEER (AS THE BRUERY HAS A LARGE BOURBON BARREL AGING PROGRAM), MOST OF THEIR BOURBON CHARACTER IS GONE, BUT IT'S A NICE WAY TO GIVE THE BARRELS A NEW LIFE!	

TASTE THIS RUSSIAN RIVER SUPPLICATION	FLAVOUR SOUR, FUNKY, CHERRY, VINOUS	ABV 7%
(STYLE) WILD SPECIALTY BEER **ORIGIN** SANTA ROSA, CALIFORNIA, USA	**NOTES** THIS BROWN ALE IS AGED ON CHERRIES IN PINOT NOIR BARRELS CONTAINING WILD YEAST AND BACTERIA. BRETT IS INTRODUCED FIRST, THEN A FEW WEEKS OR MONTHS LATER, A MIXED CULTURE OF BACTERIA IS ADDED, AND THE BARRELS AGE FOR ANOTHER SIX TO 12 MONTHS. THERE ARE LAYERS OF COMPLEXITY: A SOUR EDGE, FOLLOWED BY FRUIT AND WINE NOTES.	

CHAPTER
6
SIX

1200s–1980s

A WORD
ON WHEAT

While wheat and barley were domesticated around the same time, approximately 7000 BCE, divisions were formed early on. Wheat was for the bakers and barley for the brewers because each was uniquely suited to its intended use.

We've sung barley's praises for brewing before – it's relatively low in protein, full of starches and the enzymes needed to convert them to sugars and has an outer husk that helps with filtration. As wheat is higher in protein and doesn't have an outer husk, it's rather difficult to brew with, as it gets gummy and makes the mash hard to drain.

(That said, it's the proteins in wheat that help give bread its texture. Bake with barley alone and you'd get bread that's dry, hard and crumbly. It's no wonder those baking–brewing divisions formed early!)

While it would be very difficult to produce a beer using only wheat, many brewers blurred the lines and brewed beers with a blend of wheat and barley. We've seen this as far back as the 13th century with the hoppy wheat beers brewed by the Hanseatic League.

In the early days, these styles likely would have been brewed with air-dried malt and unmalted wheat, giving them their lightly coloured, hazy appearance and the nickname "white beers" (*witbier* in Belgium, or *weissbier* in Germany).

As wheat was crucial for bakers and has rather specific growing conditions, making it challenging to produce, there were often tight controls on wheat's use in brewing. Some countries prohibited it altogether.

With competition for the key ingredient and a flood of mass-market pale lager redefining beer, it's easy to see how these styles could fall out of favour if they're not protected. Incredibly, for the styles that survived, it's often a single individual responsible whose stories you're about to learn.

WHEAT BEER GOES WAY BACK
1200s

Hazy, white beers date as far back as the 13th century to the days of the Hanseatic League along the North Sea. If you'll recall from Chapter Four, the first hopped beer was white, or wheat-based, beer from Hamburg that was shipped out by sea and helped spur the adoption of hops.

It's important to keep in mind that at this time Germany wasn't yet a unified country. Back then, each state or principality had its own laws, customs and regional brewing styles*. So while brewers in Bavaria were limited to barley, water and hops from 1516 on, those restrictions didn't apply elsewhere.

Although spices and acidity are most often associated with Belgian brewing traditions, northern Germany had a long and varied brewing history similar to that of Belgium, including a tradition of brewing with wheat.

The north German town of Goslar gave one of these ancient wheat beer styles its name – gose. Originating there in the Middle Ages, gose later became associated with the nearby town of Leipzig in the 18th century.

This sour wheat-based beer is brewed with both pilsner and wheat malt, fermented by brewer's yeast and Lactobacillus, which gives it a bright acidity, and spiced with coriander and sea salt. The coriander contributes a lemony freshness, while the salt gives the beer a feeling of fullness on the palate. (It's thought the initial brewing water from the Gose River was a bit salty, which then became the standard for the style.)

In the past, this style was likely soured by spontaneous fermentation, creating a sharp acidity that was blunted by the addition of fruit or herbal syrups, like Kummel (a liqueur flavoured with caraway, cumin and fennel) to help sweeten the beer.

Sadly, after the wars took a toll on Germany, gose production dwindled and ceased entirely in 1966. Since the 1980s, a few local breweries in Leipzig have sought to revive the style. But with no continuity in brewing, what we're drinking today is our best approximation.

For example, today's interpretations are likely more restrained in acidity, as Lactobacillus is introduced and its acid production can be controlled, unlike the spontaneous fermentations of the past.

In all, gose is light, tart, spritzy, citrusy and incredibly refreshing. But it's also hard to find.

Leipzig was said to have over 80 gose houses in the 1900s. Today, there's

>>

one. But it's well worth a visit to immerse yourself in the traditions of this style – from the serve in tall cylindrical glasses, to the shot of syrup on the side. (Check out my recommended places to visit in the Conclusion.)

Slightly further north, Berlin has its own wheat beer tradition that also derives from the early white beers of the North Sea. In many ways, it's very similar to a *gose*, but is brewed without any additional spices.

Berliner *weisse* is also fermented with yeast and lactic acid bacteria, giving it a sharp, yogurt-like tang, citrusy freshness and high carbonation. The wheat malt gives a bready, doughy note, making the flavour almost reminiscent of sourdough bread. (*Brettanomyces* may also be use in the brew, but its character is never strong.)

Because of its high carbonation, Napoleon is said to have dubbed this style the "Champagne of the North" when the Franco–Prussian war brought him and his men to Berlin in the early 1800s. Much like *gose*, traditional Berliner *weisse* was also served with a shot of sugar syrup on the side, often flavoured with raspberry or woodruff.

From the height of its popularity, there is only one traditional example left, Berliner Kindl Weisse, which dates back to the style's 19th century heyday. A few new breweries in Berlin are working to revive this style, albeit on a small scale.

Although traditional examples are hard to come by outside of Berlin, many craft breweries in the USA and UK are giving this style a go. So check your local brewery to see if they're producing one.

While what we experience of these styles today may not be truly traditional, it's better than losing them forever.

* Fortunately, even after German unification in 1871, special exceptions were made for these regional styles so they could continue being brewed even if they didn't meet the Bavarian beer purity law.

TASTE THIS BAYERISCHER BAHNHOF LEIPZIGER GOSE	FLAVOUR SLIGHTLY SOUR, SPRITZY, REFRESHING	ABV 4.5%
(STYLE) GOSE **ORIGIN** LEIPZIG, GERMANY	**NOTES** THIS BREWERY OPENED IN THE EARLY 2000S AND IS ONE OF ONLY THREE IN THE LEIPZIG AREA PRODUCING THE HISTORIC GOSE STYLE. WHO KNOWS HOW WELL IT APPROXIMATES THE REAL THING, BUT IT'S AS CLOSE AS WE'LL GET TO A TASTE OF HISTORY.	

NO LONGER JUST FOR BAVARIAN ROYALTY
1872

Now, we move on to what most people think of as German wheat beer – *hefeweizen* or German *weissbier*.

The southern German state of Bavaria has brewed wheat beer for hundreds of years, but following the *Reinheitsgebot*, the use of wheat in brewing was a right reserved for Bavarian royalty only.

The Bavarian beer purity law, the *Reinheitsgebot* of 1516, stated only barley, water and hops could be used to brew beer (as yeast wasn't yet understood). And with that, the tradition of wheat beer brewing in Bavaria ceased immediately – a decision that was rather unpopular.

So in 1602, the ban on wheat was replaced with a system of special licences that allowed the licence holder to brew wheat beer. The problem? The Elector of Bavaria, who introduced the new system, bought them all for himself, giving the Bavarian royal family a monopoly on wheat beer production for the next 200-plus years.

As the style waned in popularity by the 19th century, a Munich brewer, Georg Schneider, negotiated the rights to brew this once-reserved style. In 1872, he opened his own brewery, Schneider Weisse, which is still world famous for its wheat beer today.

As discussed in Chapter Five, what makes German wheat beer so unique is its yeast – it adds aromas of banana, bubble gum and clove. But it's also brewed with at least 50% wheat malt (some up to 70%), which changes the composition and mouthfeel of the beer quite significantly.

Weissbier means white beer, while *weizenbier* means wheat beer. It's a small distinction, but an important one. Why? Despite the historic family name – white beers – not all wheat beers are pale. Many are yellow to gold, while some are deep gold, nearly amber.

The original from Schneider Weisse, Tap 7, is a darker example and a true taste of history.

Around the 1960s, pale *weissbiers* became more popular, hence why examples from Weihenstephaner and Erdinger are lighter in colour than Schneider Weisse. It's largely personal preference, so I'd say give them all a go to find your favourite.

A broad term encompassing the various shades and strengths of German wheat beer, the name *weissbier* has more to do with the hazy appearance of the beer than the colour. The haze comes from wheat's high protein content and the fact the yeast isn't filtered from the beer, meaning it's suspended in the glass as

>>

you drink. (This is where the style's alternative name comes from. *"Hefe"* means yeast and *"weizen"* means wheat. That said, there is a filtered version available, called *kristalweizen*, for any purists out there.)

As the yeast is still in the beer when it's bottled, it will continue to consume any available sugars, enhancing the beer's carbonation.

Combined with the beer's high protein content, the carbonation gives German wheat beers a creamy body and a mousse-like head that resembles a meringue. So fluffy and creamy, the style has its own special glassware – a *weissbier* vase – to contain all the foam.

There are several variations, from both pale and dark, to stronger versions, like *weizenbocks* (which you tried back in Chapter Four, Schneider Weisse Tap 5). All can be identified by their distinct aromas of banana and clove and their beautiful milkshake-like appearance.

If you're a fan of this style, you now know who to thank for bringing it back. Similarly, one individual is credited with reviving Belgium's wheat beer style. Read on to learn his story.

TASTE THIS SCHNEIDER WEISSE ORIGINAL TAP 7	FLAVOUR BANANA, BUBBLE GUM, CLOVE, BREADY MALT	ABV 5.4%
(STYLE) GERMAN WEISSBIER **ORIGIN** MUNICH, GERMANY	**NOTES** THE ORIGINAL FROM 1872, THIS BEER TAKES ON A DEEP AMBER COLOUR AND THE AROMAS OF BANANA AND CLOVE JUMP OUT OF THE GLASS, HELPED BY THE BEER'S HIGH CARBONATION. LOOKING FOR SOMETHING LIGHTER? TRY A PALE VERSION (TAP 1) OR EVEN A FILTERED KRISTALWEIZEN (TAP 2).	

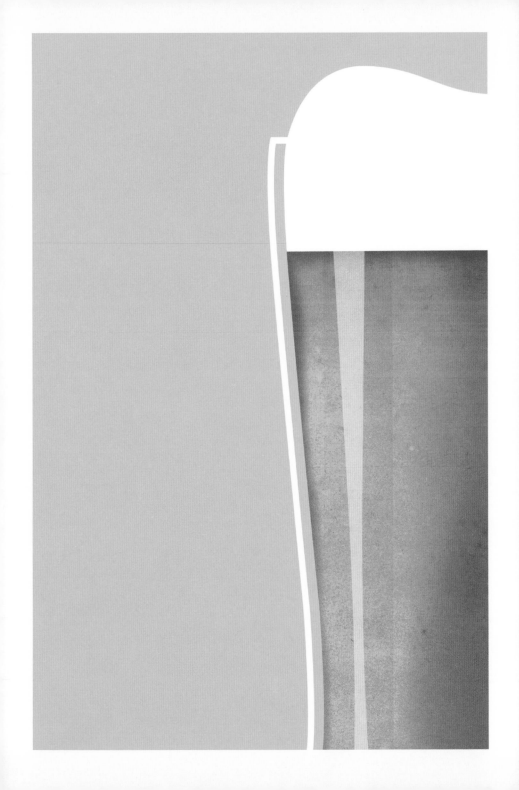

A 400-YEAR-OLD RECIPE REVIVED
1960s

Never experiencing a purity law like Germany, the Belgian tradition of brewing with spices – and whatever's available, really – is well exemplified by Belgian wheat beer, or *witbier*.

With roots as far back as the Middle Ages from the same white beer family as the German styles we've just discussed, *witbier* took its present form in the 1500s when the spice trade introduced brewers to its now-characteristic flavours.

Unlike German wheat beer, Belgian wheat beer is brewed with unmalted wheat, which contributes to the beer's cloudiness. The beer is typically 50% unmalted wheat and 50% barley malt but may also include a small portion of raw oats.

Belgium had some unique laws over the years that also significantly impacted their brewing styles.

In 1822, brewers were taxed based on the capacity of their mash tun (the container that holds your malt and brewing liquor for the mashing process), but could have a second tun for unmalted grains that was not taxed.

So they'd jam-pack their mash tun in a way that would extract lots of long-chain sugars (called dextrins) and use loads of unmalted grains, like unmalted wheat. This approach to mashing, called a turbid mash, contributes to Belgian *witbier's* cloudy appearance and creamy body. (This process is also used in lambic beers, as the dextrins become energy sources for wild yeast and bacteria. Additionally, it's a much more complex process than I've laid out here!)

Traditional spicing of a *witbier* includes bitter orange peel and coriander seed (which we also saw used in the *gose*). It's said many Belgian brewers also use secret spices, thought to be anything from chamomile to grains of paradise.

The key distinction here is the fruit and spice in a Belgian *witbier* come from the addition of those ingredients, while the fruit and spice in a German *weizenbier* is all from the yeast.

Belgian *witbiers* are refreshing, elegant and of moderate strength. They're effervescent with notes of fruit and spice, minimal bitterness and a dry, tart finish. Again, yeast and wheat contribute the haze, hence the name white beer.

At its peak in the 18th century, Hoegaarden, one of two Belgian towns best known for brewing *witbier,* had over 30 breweries. War, brewery consolidations and competition from the popularity of pilsner-style beers weren't kind to Belgian *witbier* though. It fell out of fashion and by the 1950s all Belgian *witbier* production had ceased.

But in 1966, Pierre Celis, a local milkman, who worked at a *witbier* brewery when he was younger, set up his own brewery to bring back the style. Naming the beer after the town, he called it Hoegaarden.

Any chance the name sounds familiar? The brewery was later sold to Belgian brewing giant Interbrew, now Anheuser-Busch InBev, and Hoegaarden can be found throughout the world.

Without Pierre's effort, the style could have been lost. And sadly, there are plenty of other regional styles that haven't been saved. But all it takes is for some creative craft brewers to go digging through old brewing texts to find more styles to revive or reinvent.

TASTE THIS	FLAVOUR	ABV
HOEGAARDEN	CITRUS, SPICE, REFRESHING, CRISP	4.9%
(STYLE)		
BELGIAN WIT	**NOTES**	
	DON'T ADJUST YOUR SET, THIS BEER IS MEANT TO BE CLOUDY	
ORIGIN	THANKS TO ALL THAT WHEAT. YOU'LL TASTE SWEETNESS FROM	
HOEGAARDEN, BELGIUM	THE WHEAT, CITRUS ZEST FROM THE ORANGE PEEL AND A	
	HERBAL FRESHNESS FROM THE CORIANDER.	

THE AMERICAN TAKE
1980s

German brewers brought their versions of wheat beer (both *hefeweizen* and Berliner *weisse*) with them as they emigrated to the USA in the late 1800s, so the country has had a slightly more storied wheat beer history than this timeline makes it appear. But sadly, none of those styles survived Prohibition.

What we think of today as American wheat beer is the craft beer adaptation popularized by the Widmer Brewery of Portland, Oregon, in the 1980s.

It's like a German wheat beer, but without the emphasis on yeast. Instead, a cleaner ale yeast is used, and a citrusy character is introduced from citrusy, piney hops instead. There's no banana or clove here.

Fun fact: this change was likely driven by necessity in the early days of craft brewing. Instead of maintaining multiple yeast strains, like the one responsible for the German *weissbier*, most craft breweries were too concerned about infections and just used the same style for all beers. (Rightly enough; an IPA that tastes of banana and clove might be a bit off-putting!)

Driven more by the wheat character than the yeast, this style is creamy, lightly grainy and has a nice amount of hop bitterness. Unlike most German styles, which have 50% wheat, American styles are typically between 30 and 50%. But they're still served unfiltered with a slight haze.

Not nearly as characterful as the German or Belgian versions, American wheat beer is often seen as a "gateway" beer used to introduce new drinkers to wheat-based styles. Got a friend who needs a little convincing to give beer a go? Start them on an American wheat beer and see if that helps.

(Then once they've discovered their love for beer, you've got the perfect book to recommend to help them learn more about it!)

TASTE THIS WIDMER HEFE	FLAVOUR CITRUS, BREADY, REFRESHING	ABV 4.9%
(STYLE) AMERICAN WHEAT BEER		
ORIGIN PORTLAND, OREGON, USA	**NOTES** YES, IT HAS GOT HEFEWEIZEN ON THE LABEL, BUT YOU KNOW WELL BY NOW THAT'S MORE OF A NOD TO ITS INSPIRATION THAN A DESCRIPTOR OF THIS STYLE. BREWED WITH A CLEANER YEAST, THIS BEER IS WHEATY AND FRUITY, BUT HAS NO BANANA OR CLOVES.	

CONCLUSION:
INNOVATION
CONTINUES

We made it! Thanks so much for joining me on this journey through beer's evolution, learning the stories of more than 50 beer styles.

But we're not quite finished yet. Always looking towards what's new and what's next, it's unsurprising that brewers continue to innovate.

We'll start with an easy idea – that of "Americanizing" a traditional European beer style. (Essentially, the US version will be more hop-forward, as American craft brewers can't get enough of their hops, but we'll go into a bit more detail.)

Next we'll talk through three different areas of innovation today – the use of different spices and flavourings, the range of grains used to brew and the very popular trend of aging beers in barrels that previously held wine and spirits.

Finally, we'll end with a list of recommended books to read and places to see, should you want to go and learn more about any of the topics we've discussed.

In all, I hope I've left you feeling inspired to learn more and that with each sip, the broad range of beer styles available today has started to make a bit more sense.

AMERICANIZATION

There are a few remaining styles I haven't gone into detail on, largely because they're American craft beer versions of a traditional English style.

When the craft beer movement first kicked off in the US, the only home brew texts available were from British writers, hence why many American homebrewers had an early British influence.

As you've read, most modern American interpretations of traditional British styles can be best summed up by their shared characteristics – they are always more hop-forward, more robust in flavour and typically a bit higher in strength too. For example, American pale ale and American IPA are much more bitter and hop-forward compared to their English inspirations (as discussed in Chapter Four).

Here's a quick rundown of other "Americanized" styles:

- American amber ale – This style was developed during the modern craft beer era as an alternative to the American pale ale. It's a bit more malt-forward, often from the inclusion of dark caramel malts or other roasted malts, but it's still heavily hopped. The malt character means the style has a less bitter balance. If you're finding American pale ale too bitter, give an amber ale a try.

- American brown ale – Essentially a British brown ale with more hops, this style got its start thanks to Pete's Wicked Ale, first brewed by early craft beer pioneer Pete's Brewing Company in 1986. Although the beer is no longer around, others have picked up the mantle, producing a brown beer with a nutty, toasty character and heaps of hops. Best described as "malty but hoppy", the hops complement the beer's chocolate and caramel notes. My personal favourite is Maduro from Cigar City.

- American porter and stout – A stronger, more aggressive version of the English porter or Irish stout, both of these beers will be more bitter than their inspirations. That said, the stout will still be stronger and more robust than the porter with richer roast character, which can boost the beer's overall bitterness. (Note: compared to a black IPA, an American stout will have more malt body and roast character.)

- American barleywine – Take a strong English barleywine and up the hopping rates but keep the malt presence there. American barleywines are still strong, rich and made for sipping, but have more bitterness in the balance. Best exemplified by Sierra Nevada Bigfoot Barleywine, first brewed in 1983.

The main exceptions to the rule, of course, are the American lager and light lager, which are much thinner in hop character, bitterness and body than their European counterparts. That said though, American craft brewers have come up with all kinds of creative names to describe their hop-forward takes on German and Czech lagers, from "India pale lager" to "hoppy pilsner".

In 2018, the Brewers Association added "Contemporary American-Style Pilsner" to the judging line-up for the Great American Beer Festival, so we'll see if the BCJP guidelines include something similar in their next revision.

The other exception is the American blonde ale, which is less hop-forward than the British version, British golden ale. American blonde ales are seen as "gateway" beers to get people into craft beer so are generally more malt-oriented, but hops are definitely still present.

SUGAR AND SPICE

Historically, a wide range of additional ingredients were used to brew – beyond barley and before hops.

The Picts, ancient occupants of the British Isles, brewed beer containing heather, while some brewers along the North Sea brewed with juniper, a tradition still seen today in some Finnish farmhouse styles.

Although the days of gruit are long gone, herbs and spices still play an important role in some classic Belgian styles, like *witbier* and *saison*.

Always interested in ways to amp up flavour, American craft brewers have taken up the mantle when it comes to brewing with various different herbs, spices, sugars and more.

Sometimes they're guided by the seasons, like with the pumpkin ales that pop up on US shelves the weeks and months before Thanksgiving. Often using an American amber or brown ale as a base, the beer may be sweetened with brown sugar or maple syrup, then spiced to taste like a pumpkin pie using cinnamon, allspice, nutmeg and ginger – some even include actual pumpkin! You may also find strong winter warmers that are nicely spiced, reminiscent of anything from mulled wine spices to Christmas pudding.

Other fruits, vegetables, spices and herbs aren't out of the question. Fruits like raspberry and blueberry often find their way into American wheat beers. Herbs and spices, from tea, coffee, chocolate and chili peppers, have been included in all kinds of styles, from Earl Grey IPAs to imperial chocolate and chili stouts.

Sugars can be added into the brew for various reasons (perhaps to increase the alcohol content or thin out the body of the beer), but they may also be used to add flavour, as maple syrup, molasses and honey have plenty of rich flavour compounds to contribute, in addition to being a sugar source.

In some cases, the sugar might be used to change the mouthfeel of the beer, like with lactose in milk stouts. As yeast can't ferment this sugar, it remains in the finished beer, making the beer sweeter and smoother.

If you can believe it, some brewers have added lactose, along with fruit puree, into their IPAs to create "milkshake IPAs". I told you there's still plenty of room for innovation!

A RANGE
OF GRAINS

You're well aware by now that barley is the main grain used for brewing, but wheat played an important role in historical styles, from Germany to Belgium and the USA.

Beyond barley and wheat though, many other grains have been used in the past, from buckwheat and sorghum to emmer and millet. Some were out of necessity, but others are used today as a way to introduce new textures and flavours.

These days, you wouldn't find a brewer producing a beer using only oats, as they're quite gummy and sticky, making it hard to drain off the sweet wort after mashing. Used in small proportions though, oats add a smooth, silky body to a beer.

We mentioned oats back in Chapter One when discussing oatmeal stouts, but oats have now found their way into styles like British bitter and *kölsch*-style ales as they offer proteins that help support the head of foam on a beer.

Rye has a long history in certain German and Finnish styles. *Roggenbier* is essentially a *dunkelweizen* or dark wheat beer that's exchanged malted rye for malted wheat. All of the banana, bubble gum and clove character from the yeast is still present, but the rye contributes more spice, almost like pumpernickel bread. The Finnish

farmhouse ale, *sahti*, brewed for special occasions, is produced with rye, along with juniper branches and juniper berries.

If you find it in a craft beer these days, it's likely that rye will be used in a much smaller proportion than the Germans or Finns used, but again, it helps to add a bit of body and a balanced spice. It's popular in IPAs as the rye spice works well with citrusy hop notes.

Brewers may choose to alter their fermentables to produce a gluten-free beer by brewing with gluten-free grains like sorghum and buckwheat. Alternatively, beer can be brewed with traditional grains, then the gluten can be reduced with the help of an enzyme that breaks it down.

I wanted to circle back to barley once more before we go, because with beer's other three ingredients, our story brought us to the present day. We can edit water chemistry, breed new hop varietals, and select and pitch any isolated yeast or bacteria strain. But we left off with malt at the end of the 19th century.

Impressively, all of the malts that came about in the 19th century – pilsner, pale ale, Vienna, Munich and crystal/caramel – are still in use today!

Production methods have of course improved, enabling maltsters to make more consistent, fine-tuned batches – as malt production is all about precise control of moisture levels, time in the kiln and temperature – but the basics were all there in the 1800s. These days, maltsters can produce crystal or caramel malts with a specific colour, for example: Caramel 10 is 10 Lovibond, while Caramel 80 – you guessed it – registers precisely at 80 on the Lovibond scale. (If you recall back in Chapter One, Joseph Lovibond introduced this scale to measure beer colour in the 1880s.)

The major change to malt has been the barley breeding programs that began in the 1950s. While hop breeding introduces new aromas and flavours, barley breeders are looking for grains more suitable for malting (high yield, pest and disease resistance, low protein content, high water uptake, etc.). New barley varietals won't necessarily have a big flavour impact for the drinker, but know there is still plenty going on with barley behind the scenes.

BOOZY BARRELS

Ever since their invention more than 2,000 years ago, wooden barrels have played a crucial role in the storage, transport and dispense of beer, wine and spirits.

While many wines and spirits pick up key flavour characteristics from the wooden barrels they age in, brewers would often go to great lengths to prevent their barrels from influencing beer's flavour. They'd source fine-grained wood that wouldn't give off any flavour, scrub down the vats, or line their barrels with "brewer's pitch" to provide a water-tight coating.

Beyond imparting flavour, wood can also harbour microorganisms and is difficult to keep clean. The mature vinous notes in long-aged "stale" porter from wild yeast *Brettanomyces* might be considered desirable to some, but wood can also harbour cultures of souring bacteria. And unless you're a producer of lambic or Flanders red, you probably don't want that bacteria anywhere near your beer.

So it's no wonder that when stainless steel kegs finally came about after World War II, wooden barrels largely saw the end of their use in the brewing industry (with the exception of the sour styles previously mentioned), as kegs didn't impart any flavour to the finished beer and were much easier to keep clean.

In the 1990s, however, American craft brewers began to experiment with wood once again: some for its souring properties, bringing the Belgian sour and wild ale traditions to the USA, while others used barrels to impart totally different flavours – the flavours of the wine and spirits the barrels used to hold.

Barrel aging can impact beer's flavour in several ways. As mentioned earlier, beer can pick up flavours from the wood itself, like vanilla and oak. Additionally, because barrels are porous, the movement of oxygen allows for oxidative flavours to develop. While some of these flavours are unwelcome (think papery and wet cardboard), others can be quite pleasant, almost sherry-like. But the main flavour impact in these beers comes from whatever wine or spirit was in the barrel first.

Goose Island Brewing Company in Chicago is often credited as the first brewery to commercially produce a barrel-aged beer after they aged a stout in wooden barrels that had previously held bourbon. (Back in 1992, they had six bourbon barrels. Today, they have thousands.) As all bourbon must be aged in new oak, once used the barrels are useless to the bourbon makers, and relatively cheap for the breweries looking to experiment. (Or at least they were when this style was first introduced!)

From the early days of bourbon, breweries soon began to experiment with wine barrels, then all kinds of other spirits, from tequila and rum to gin. The key is to choose a beer style that will stand up to the flavour, and alcohol, imparted by the wood – whether it's wine or spirits. That said, it's often strong, dark imperial stouts or barley wines, but strong golden ales have been aged too.

Just like the use of barrels for sour and wild ales, brewers will likely age multiple barrels, then blend them before releasing the finished product. Balance is key to this style; barrel aged beers should taste smooth, flavourful and well-aged.

First categorized as a beer style by the Brewer's Association at the 2002 Great American Beer Festival, the Wood or Barrel-Aged Beer category had 26 entries. In 2018, there were over 400.

There's so much room for experimentation with this style, you can bet it will be around a while.

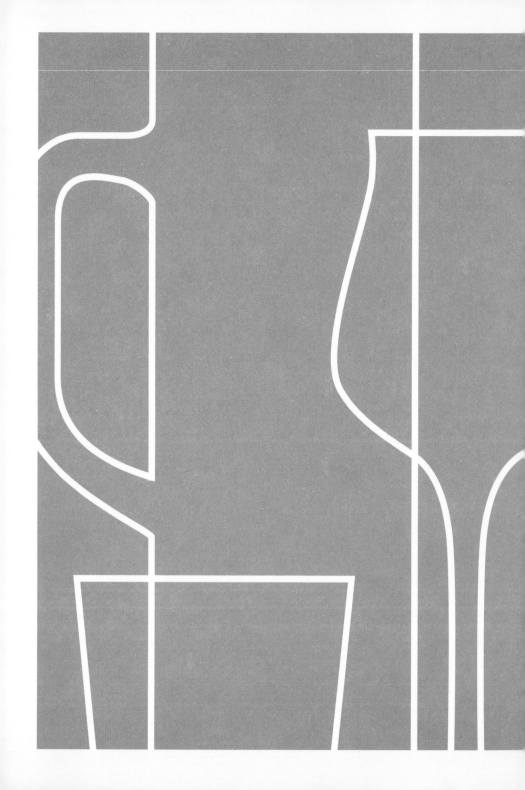

FURTHER READING

Ready to learn more? Beer history is
so rich and fascinating and this is just
a little taste. Below, I've included a few
books I'd recommend getting stuck
into next. I've also created a shortlist
of a dozen breweries or other beer-
related places to visit, some of which
feel like a trip back in time.

If you're looking for any other
recommendations or further
information, don't hesitate to be
in touch!

MIRACLE BREW
by Pete Brown

LAGER
by Dave Carpenter

AMBER, GOLD, AND BLACK
by Martyn Cornell

A BRIEF HISTORY OF LAGER
by Mark Dredge

TASTING BEER
by Randy Mosher

THE BREWMASTER'S TABLE
by Garrett Oliver

There are of course plenty of other
books I've referenced while writing,
which you can find in the bibliography.
(The above are more history-focused,
while others are a bit more technical.)

WHERE TO VISIT

I've included a selection of some of my favourite places to visit for a proper taste of history. To include them all would require another book, but if you are looking for more inspiration, check out Mark Dredge's *Beer Bucket List* or Stephen Beaumont's *Will Travel for Beer*. Happy exploring!

PILSNER URQUELL BREWERY
IN PILSEN, CZECH REPUBLIC

While their brewing process has modernized with the times, Pilsner Urquell still produces beer using more traditional methods on a much smaller scale. This practice, called parallel brewing, enables brewers to ensure that by modernizing their methods they're not changing the flavour of the beer. Beer still ferments and conditions in wooden barrels in the cellars below the brewery, just like it would have nearly 200 years ago. And if you take a tour, you can have a taste! This unfiltered, unpasteurized Pilsner Urquell tapped directly from a wooden barrel in the brewery's cellars is an experience not to be missed.

GOSENSCHENKE OHNE BEDENKEN
IN LEIPZIG, GERMANY

The last remaining gose house in Leipzig, Ohne Bedenken is as close as we'll get to a taste of this style's history. The two local brands of gose, Leipziger and Ritterguts, can be purchased here, and in 2017, the bar started brewing their own, Edelgose. Here gose is still served in the traditional way, in tall cylindrical glass, often with a shot of cherry or caraway syrup on the side.

PÄFFGEN BREWERY
IN COLOGNE, GERMANY

There are many tap houses in Cologne where you can enjoy the bigger brands of kölsch, but for a truly authentic experience, visit Päffgen, Cologne's oldest brewery. One long building on the outskirts of the city's old town, the beer is brewed on-site at the back of the building, so it doesn't have to travel far to reach the brew hall up front! Here, there's no bar to order from; it's all table service and there's one single draught beer. Take a seat and a waiter will stop by and drop off a stange full of freshly poured *kölsch*. Ever so attentively, an empty glass is replaced with a full one almost immediately as your total is tallied up on a coaster.

ZUM UERIGE
IN DÜSSELDORF, GERMANY

Düsseldorf is just a short train ride from Cologne, so you can enjoy both *altbier* and *kölsch* on the same trip. *Altbier* is best enjoyed in the Altstadt, the old town of Düsseldorf. Zum Uerige is one of several brewpubs in the old town, but it's one of my favourites because of its bustling vibe and delicious beer. If you didn't get your fix of the serving style in Cologne, *altbier* is also served in small stange glasses, round after round. Had enough? Place your coaster over the top of your empty glass, the sign you're ready to go. Otherwise, the beers will just keep coming. (Which isn't necessarily a bad thing!)

AUGUSTINER-KELLER
IN MUNICH, GERMANY

Augustiner makes some of Munich's best beers and they're certainly best enjoyed here. In the summer, the outdoor beer garden seats nearly 5,000. Even if you visit in winter though, there's plenty of room inside the massive beer hall. You can even go downstairs to their former cellars, where the beer used to keep cool while fermenting and conditioning. The scale is pretty impressive! There's a range of lagers to try and the pretzels are a must.

SCHLENKERLA
IN BAMBERG, GERMANY

Most of us are only familiar with smoked beer as a bottled product, but give it a go on draught at Schlenkerla and it's much lighter, sweeter, and surprisingly quite refreshing. I could only have one pint (that said, that was just after one other pint around the corner at Spezial!), but even if you do order just one, sip and savour it while you soak up your surroundings. This historic tavern is draped in dark wood, cosy with conversation and cooks up plenty of delicious German delicacies.

RODENBACH BREWERY
IN ROESELARE, BELGIUM

Ready to be awed? Visit Rodenbach. Their cellars house nearly 300 oak foeders, each holding thousands of litres of beer. While they use a much more modern brew house today, you can walk through the maltings, see the old copper fermenters and of course sample their range of beers and blends among the foeders.

CANTILLON BREWERY
IN BRUSSELS, BELGIUM

A true step back in time, Cantillon Brewery was established in Brussels in 1901 and still brews there to this day. Much like a museum, you can take a self-guided or guided tour around the brewery, learning about the coolship, the barrels and how the beers are blended. Afterwards, sample straight lambic poured uncarbonated from a pitcher or stick around and share a bottle of *gueuze* or one of their many fruit lambics.

NATIONAL BREWERY CENTRE MUSEUM
IN BURTON UPON TRENT, ENGLAND

Although Burton was once the world's biggest brewing centre, its history is well hidden. Today, many British breweries are still based in Burton, but the brands of old are long gone. To learn more about the city's rich brewing history, visit the National Brewery Centre Museum and immerse yourself in it. Then walk across town for a pint at the historic Coopers Tavern, which has been around since the 1800s and the heyday of Bass Brewery.

THE HARP PUB
IN LONDON, ENGLAND

Known as one of London's premier pubs for cask beer, The Harp shouldn't be missed. A Fuller's pub, you're likely to find a range of Fuller's beers on cask alongside other British breweries both traditional and modern. As good cask beer requires care, you can trust the beers at The Harp have been well looked after.

RUSSIAN RIVER BREWPUB
IN SANTA ROSA, CALIFORNIA

Russian River has perfected two very diverse beer styles. Well known for both their style-defining double IPA, Pliny the Elder, and for their innovative American wild ales, there's something for any beer lover here. Can't decide?

Try their sampler to taste everything that's on tap. And once you've made it to the Bay Area, why not check out a few other local breweries? There's plenty of great beer to be found nearby, so be sure to explore.

SIERRA NEVADA
IN ASHEVILLE, NORTH CAROLINA

Yes, Sierra Nevada got its start in Chico, California, but in 2015 they built a second facility on the East Coast to be better positioned to supply customers on the other side of the States and across the Atlantic. And I have to say, the facility is truly epic. It shows just how far Sierra Nevada has come since the earliest days of the craft beer movement it helped kick off. Here you can taste all of their West Coast classics alongside their new innovations.

BIBLIOGRAPHY

Acitelli, Tom, *The Audacity of Hops: The History of America's Craft Beer Revolution*, Chicago Review Press, Chicago, 2013

Allen, Fal, *Gose: Brewing a Classic German Beer for the Modern Era*, Brewers Publications, Boulder, 2018

Alworth, Jeff, "Quirks of Brewing: Parti-gyle Brewing", *All About Beer*, 2015, accessed at www.allaboutbeer.com/quirks-of-brewing-parti-gyle-brewing

Anchor Brewery, "Anchor Steam Beer", accessed at www.anchorbrewing.com/beer/anchor_steam

Beer & Cider Academy, "Foundation Course", course slides, 2019

Beer Judge Certification Program, "How did we get our start?", www.bjcp.org/history.php

Brewers Association, "Number of Breweries", accessed at www.brewersassociation.org/statistics/number-of-breweries

Brewers Association Beer Style Guidelines 2018 Edition, www.brewersassociation.org/resources/brewers-association-beer-style-guidelines

British Hop Association, "Fuggle", accessed at www.britishhops.org.uk/varieties/fuggle

British Hop Association, "Goldings", accessed at www.britishhops.org.uk/varieties/goldings

British Stainless Steel Association, "The History of Stainless Steel", www.bssa.org.uk/about_stainless_steel.php?id=124

Brooklyn Brewery, "Brooklyn Lager", accessed at http://brooklynbrewery.com/brooklyn-beers/perennial-brews/brooklyn-lager

Brown, Pete, *Miracle Brew: Hops, Barley, Water, Yeast, and the Nature of Beer*, Unbound, London 2017

Cantwell, Dick and Bouckaert, Peter, *Wood & Beer: A Brewer's Guide*, Brewers Publications, Boulder, 2016

Carpenter, Dave, *Lager: The Definitive Guide to Tasting and Brewing the World's Most Popular Beer Styles*, Quarto Publishing, Minneapolis, 2017

Cerveza Modelo, "Negra", accessed at www.modelousa.com/en-US/product/negra

Cole, Melissa, *The Little Book of Craft Beer*, Hardie Grant Books, London, 2017

Cicerone® Certification Program, "US Certified Cicerone ® Syllabus, Nov 2017", 2017 www.cicerone.org/sites/default/files/certification-syllabi/US_English_CC_Syllabus_V3.2.pdf

Cornell, Martyn, "A Short History of Hops", blog post at http://zythophile.co.uk/2009/11/20/a-short-history-of-hops/

Cornell, Martyn, "Michael Jackson and the Invention of Beer Style", blog post at http://zythophile.co.uk/2010/10/23/michael-jackson-and-the-invention-of-beer-style/

Cornell, Martyn, "So you think you know what porter tastes like", blog post at http://zythophile.co.uk/2010/04/14/so-you-think-you-know-what-porter-tastes-like/

Cornell, Martyn, "The earliest use of the term India Pale Ale was... in Australia?", blog post at http://zythophile.co.uk/2013/05/14/the-earliest-use-of-the-term-india-pale-ale-was-in-australia/

Cornell, Martyn, "The Porter Brewer and the Peterloo Massacre", blog post at http://zythophile.co.uk/2018/11/22/the-porter-brewer-and-the-peterloo-massacre/

Cornell, Martyn, *Amber, Gold, & Black*, The History Press, Stroud, 2010

Craftbeer.com, "Gluten-Free Beer", accessed at www.craftbeer.com/styles/gluten-free

Dredge, Mark, *A Brief History of Lager*, Kyle Books, London, 2019

DSM, "Brewers Clarex", www.dsm.com/markets/food-specialties/en/products/beverage/brewers-clarex.html

European Commission Agriculture and Rural Development, "Kölsch", accessed at http://ec.europa.eu/agriculture/quality/door/list.html

Official Journal of the European Communities, "Application for Registration of a Specific Product: Lambic, Gueuze-Lambic, Gueuze" accessed at https://eur-lex.europa.eu/LexUriServ/LexUriServ.do?uri=OJ:C:1997:021:0013:0014:EN:PDF

Great American Beer Festival, Past Winners, www.greatamericanbeerfestival.com/the-competition/past-winners/

Heil, Meredith, "The Oral History of Heady Topper", Vinepair.com, accessed at https://vinepair.com/articles/heady-topper-beer-history/

Hieronymous, Stan, *For the Love of Hops*, Brewers Publications, Boulder, 2012

HORAL, "The Goals of HORAL", accessed at www.horal.be/en/welcome

Jackson, Michael, *Ultimate Beer*, DK Publishing, New York, 1998

Klemp, K. Florian, "Munich Dunkel", *All About Beer*, Volume 28: Issue 4, 2007, accessed at http://allaboutbeer.com/article/munich-dunkel/

Mallet, John, *Malt: A Practical Guide from Field to Brewhouse*, Brewers Publications, Boulder, 2014

Mosher, Randy, *Tasting Beer: An Insider's Guide to the World's Greatest Drink*, Storey Publishing, North Adams, 2009, second edition

Muessdoerffer, Franz, "A Comprehensive History of Beer Brewing" in *Handbook of Brewing: Processes, Technology, Markets*, 2009

Oliver, Garrett (ed.), *The Oxford Companion to Beer*, Oxford University Press, New York, 2010

Oliver, Garrett, *The Brewmaster's Table: Discovering the Pleasures of Real Beer with Real Food*, Harper Collins Publishers, New York, 2003

Palmer, John, *How to Brew: Everything You Need to Know to Brew Beer Right the First Time*, Brewers Publications, 2006

Steele, Mitch, *IPA: Brewing Techniques, Recipes, and the Evolution of India Pale Ale*, Brewers Publications, Boulder, 2012

Strong, Gordon with Kristen England, Eds. "Beer Judge Certification Program 2015 Style Guidelines: Beer Style Guidelines", Beer Judge Certification Program, 2015

Sumner, James, "Early Heat Determination in the Brewery", *Brewery History*, Issue 121 (Winter 2005)

The Haas Blog, "The BBC Pure Hop Pellet. Efficiency + Flavour", blog post at www.johnihaas.com/blog/the-bbc-pure-hop-pellet-efficiency-flavor/

Tonsmeire, Michael, *American Sour Beers: Innovative Techniques for Mixed Fermentations*, Brewers Publications, Boulder, 2014

Verdonck, Erik and Luck De Raedemaeker, *The Belgian Beer Book*, Lannoo Publishers, Tielt, 2016

White, Chris and Jamil Zainasheff, *Yeast: The Practical Guide to Beer Fermentation*, Brewers Publications, Boulder, 2010

INDEX

ACKNOWLEDGEMENTS

I have so many people to thank for helping me get to where I am today and for making this book a reality.

Starting back where it all began at Bobby G's Pizzeria in Berkeley, California – Rupinder and Ellen, I've got you and many, many pints of Deschutes Mirror Pond to thank for setting me on the path I'm on today. Additional thanks to Ellen and Dave for my copy of *How to Brew*, which I've referenced so many times over the years (including in this book).

From NYC – Evan and Marissa: thank you for welcoming me into 29er brews, it has been great to see you both on your beery journeys too. Zach Mack: thanks for always being up for a beer and a chat anytime I visited you at ABC Beer Co; it's still my favourite bar in the city! Emily and Laura: thank you for letting me be the designated beer buyer at the Happy Family office and for putting up with all my beery chat! Steph, Catherine, Maansi and Sabina (aka CaliSwag): you've been such amazing cheerleaders throughout this process. Thank you for letting me drag you to breweries across the city and country. I couldn't ask for better drinking buddies.

Here in London – Megan and Lauren: thank you for letting me crash on your couch well beyond my welcome. I'm so lucky to have such close family by my side. To the Crafty Beer Girls: you've welcomed me with open arms (as you do for all beer-loving ladies) and are such an inspiring and supportive bunch. I wouldn't be where I am in my career without you all. My V. Serious study group: I consider myself lucky to be a part of such a passionate and determined gaggle of beer geeks. The team at Duvel: thank you for supporting me in writing this book while working full-time. And to my tight-knit office team, Nick, Umi and Janneke, thank you for keeping me sane! (Full disclosure, I worked at Duvel UK while writing this book).

My latest chapter – Jess: thank you for writing your brilliant *Salad Feasts* and for inspiring and encouraging me to pen a book about my passion. You're a rising star and I consider myself lucky to say I knew you way back when. Jo, Isabel and the team at Kyle Books: thank you for believing in my idea and for making this book a reality. Sarah: I can't thank you enough for your incredible design and illustrations, they really bring the book to life. Anthony: thanks for your excellent edits and helpful feedback. Megan, Matt, Steph, Gizem, Melissa: thank you for reviewing my proposal all those months ago. Clare and Adie: you, too heard me blabbing on about my proposal on a work trip to Burton in summer 2017 and kindly treated me to a beer at the historic Coopers Tavern. Thank you! Martyn: thank you for letting me pick your brain about beer history myths and for kindly reviewing an early chapter draft. Randy Mosher, Garrett Oliver, Pete Brown, Dave Carpenter, Mark Dredge, Melissa Cole, Martyn Cornell: your books have been real inspirations to me and mine wouldn't be here today if it weren't for yours. Ray Daniels: thank you for creating the Cicerone® Certification Program and for giving me, and others in the industry, an opportunity to learn about beer and show what we know. I hope this book helps fellow candidates on their journeys. Olav Blancquaert: thank you for always having time for my (many!) questions and for arranging our visits to Liefmans, Rodenbach and Boon. Many thanks as well to Frank Boon and Belinda Eelbode for being so generous with your time and insight.

Big hugs to more family and friends around the world for their love and support: Mom, Dad, Patrick, Tony, Jeff, Darren and Yael, and so many more aunts, uncles and cousins. And to my biggest supporters closer to home: Megan, Steph, Linzi and Nigel. Nige: I can't thank you enough for how you've supported me throughout all the ups and downs of this process. Writing a book is hard. But as you've said time and time again in your endless wisdom, "It's supposed to be, or else everybody would be doing it." I'm so grateful that you, too, love beer, but see it through a totally different lens than I do. Mother Kelly's will forever hold a special place in my heart, not only because it's where I got my beery start in London, but because it's where I met you. When Granny Margaret bought me that cheesy plaque that says, "Beer will change the world. I don't know how, but it will", I had a bit of a laugh. Then upon reflection, I realized beer brought us together and that's changed my world. I love you.

BIOGRAPHY

Natalya Watson is a Beer Sommelier
and Certified Cicerone® passionate
about sharing her knowledge of beer
with others. Fascinated by the stories
she discovered during her studies,
she began hosting talks and tastings
themed around exploring beer's
evolution, which ultimately led to the
idea for this book.

Natalya's long had a knack for making
complex scientific topics accessible
and engaging for all kinds of audiences.
She studied microbiology at UCLA,
followed by a graduate degree in
public health. From there she worked
in communications and marketing for
an organic baby food company. After
deciding to follow her passion and
pursue a career in beer, she landed
the role of UK marketing manager
for renowned Belgian brewery, Duvel
Moortgat, a role she held for three
years before going freelance to focus
on beer education.

Now, Natalya regularly hosts talks and
tastings across London and beyond.
She also teaches at The Beer & Cider
Academy, judges at beer competitions,
and produces and hosts the podcast,
"Beer with Nat." Find out more at
beerwithnat.com.